HORNBY
magazine yearbook

Edited by Mike Wild

Ian Allan
PUBLISHING

Editor: Mike Wild
Sub Editor: Andrew Roden
Design: Ian Blaza
Contributors: Evan Green Hughes and Phil Parker.

First published, November 2011

ISBN 978 0 7110 3657 4

Publishing by Ian Allan Publishing

An imprint of Ian Allan Publishing Ltd, Hersham, Surrey KT12 4RG.
Printed in England by Ian Allan Publishing Ltd, Hersham, Surrey KT12 4TG

Visit the Ian Allan Publishing website at
www.ianallanpublishing.com

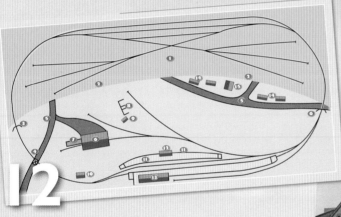

12

124

116

Welcome

Welcome to the fourth *Hornby Magazine Yearbook*. This year we've put together a quite different format for this book to illustrate the many and varied aspects of railway modelling in a new and - we hope - even more attractive way.

The theme for this Yearbook is a Western Region layout. This new project has been built by the *Hornby Magazine* team to show how simple it can be to produce a working railway. Within the remit of this layout we are offering tips, techniques, background information and more.

We choose the Western Region as the theme because it is an area which we haven't covered in great detail before. Yes, we've featured layouts and rolling stock from the Western in the magazine, but until now our team hasn't built a railway based on GWR practice.

The subject layout, St Stephens Road, is the seventh exhibition layout to be built by *Hornby Magazine* and the third in 2011 following on from the launch of Bolsover and Seven Lane Pit at Model Rail Scotland in February and our Layout in a Weekend Challenge which was tackled by a team of three at Hornby Magazine LIVE! in

Hartlepool on July 9/10.

The Western Region was, despite its critics, undoubtedly a diverse and well thought out railway system by the time of nationalisation. Churchward introduced a policy of standardisation in the early 1900s and this set the wheels in motion for an efficient operation for the next 60 years.

Our project layout is set in North Cornwall near Launceston with a junction station served by both Western Region and Southern Region trains. This captures the spirit of a busy Western branch line which carries freight and passengers while its offstage seaside terminus provides a reason for large locomotives hauling portions of express trains transporting holidaymakers from the capital to their destination.

It is always a pleasant experience to build a model railway with a purpose and St Stephens has several reasons for existence. It certainly wouldn't be the layout it is without the growing range of locomotives and rolling stock being issued and planned by the manufacturers and retailers, and it's nice to operate the increasing range of ex-GWR and Southern Railway models in something like their natural environment.

As the year approaches its end the hobby goes from strength to strength in appeal and the availability of products. Standards of detail and performance continue to rise and Digital Command Control has received a new lease of life with the arrival of Hornby's RailMaster computer control system.

This is a hobby which lives and breathes. It is never static, and that is what makes it so exciting and appealing.

From the team at *Hornby Magazine* we hope you enjoy this Yearbook as much as we have bringing it together.

Happy modelling!

Mike Wild
Editor, *Hornby Magazine*
Peterborough, September 2011

The twin Maybach engines of 'Western' hydraulic D1001 *Western Pathfinder* **idle in the station at St Stephens Road to wait for the arrival of a china clay train behind a Collett '2251' 0-6-0.** Mike Wild.

Dreaming of the perfect railway

Everyone has a perfect model railway in their mind's eye, but distilling that blurry vision into clear ideas isn't always easy. **Andrew Roden** considers what his ideal model railway might look like - and how practical considerations might shape it. *Photography, Mike Wild.*

It starts off as a muted hiss, almost lost amidst a hubbub of conversation which grows louder by the second. Then comes the sound of doors slamming shut, the sharp shriek of a whistle and then for a fraction of a second, silence as a man wearing blue overalls and a peaked cap lifts a lever in his cab. The steam from the boiler passes through the open regulator valves, racing through superheater elements before entering the steam chest. Here it can go to any of two, three or four sets of valves into a cylinder. The enormous pressure of the steam slowly but inexorably forces a piston backwards and as the piston

in turn exerts its movement on the connecting rod, the steam locomotive finally moves. The next cylinder comes into play, amplifying the forces at work and finally as the remaining steam in the cylinders is forced out of the exhaust passages into the blastpipe comes the first audible sign of life... whooof! The locomotive gradually moves away from the station, its train reluctantly at first following behind and as it gets to grips with its load the volume of the exhaust rises, defeating for a little while the doppler effect before fading into the distance.

That is one of the most compelling spectacles I have ever witnessed on the

railways, but it's not the only one. Only the most hard hearted of steam men could fail to be moved by the sound of a High Speed Train's original diesel engine straining at the leash when it leaves a station, the turbochargers howling like a million banshees screaming for release against the brakes and that beautiful streamlined body preparing to cleave its way through the air at 125mph.

We all have a favourite railway scene imprinted somewhere on our consciousness, and it's slightly different for everyone. Some are moved by the intimacy of seeing a train close up; others by zooming out and absorbing the whole spectacle. Some favour

Having the space to build our dream model railway is always the first stumbling block. This is *Hornby Magazine's* **Bay Street Shed Mk II which occupies 16ft x 9ft, but includes main line running, an extensive locomotive shed and a double track junction.**

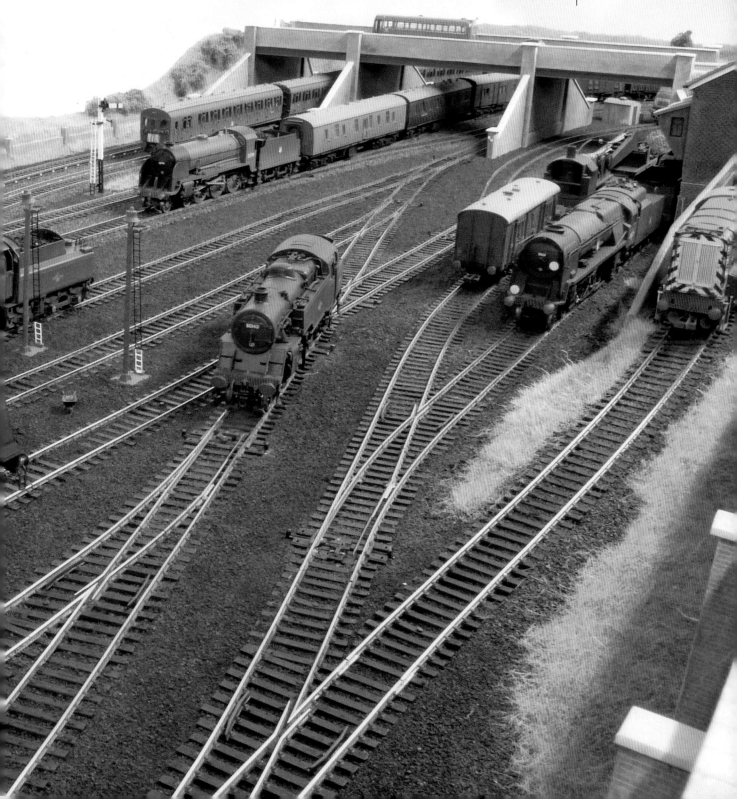

A major consideration when idealising our perfect layout is what type of trains and the region or area we want to model. A BR '9F' 2-10-0 leads a a rake of empty 20ton hopper wagons towards the colliery exchange sidings at Bolsover and Seven Lane Pit – *Hornby Magazine's* DCC exhibition layout – offering a memory of steam in the North West in the 1960s.

specific regions or periods while others have more eclectic tastes. Whatever one's preference there is something somewhere which compels us all to be interested in railways, and not surprisingly we often try to replicate it in model form.

And that poses a real problem, because even given an infinite amount of space, time and money, I doubt many of us - if anyone at all - could ever truly say they've cracked it when it comes to building the perfect model railway of their mind's eye. There are simply too many options and variables to include everything. So, given real world constraints of time, space and cost, what would my perfect model railway look like, and what would it have to include? What would be nice to have, and what would I be prepared to go without?

The essence of youth

On the basis that we often try to recapture what we remember from our youth, my mind instantly turns to Stafford in the early 1990s, when the last of the Class 81s and 85s were sharing the tracks with the then new Class 90s, and the Class 158 Diesel Multiple Units were impressing with their supreme quietness alongside elderly first generation AC Electric Multiple Units. What a spectacular layout that would be! As eclectic a mixture of trains as you'd have seen anywhere in Britain at the

time, with a mixture of express and local passenger trains, bulk and short distance freight, diesel and electric traction... and in an average house, completely and utterly impractical. Few of us would have the space to do such a scene justice and it would be a project that by its nature would have to last a lifetime.

But as well as modelling what we can remember, a lot of us model what we wish we could remember, and that for me means steam. In my mind's eye I'd like to recapture the spirit of a time when the railways mattered, when they were still the main form of transport, and when in my romanticised version of history, the trains were always clean and on time and the stations spick and span. Never mind, for a second, that the reality even in 1900 wasn't always like that - we're not dealing in reality here: this is pure fantasy, so as far as I'm concerned anything goes as long as it's consistent with itself.

The perfect layout

So what would be in my perfect model railway? If one has to be practical and confine it to a room in the house or perhaps the garage, then size isn't going to be unlimited so for real satisfaction compromises are inevitable. The starting point for me is a station. I like to give my railway purpose and a station is a reason for the trains to exist in the first place, for them to pause at or pass, and

for other activities such as shunting to take place. It doesn't have to be a big station, but if at all possible I'd like it to be significant enough to have a staff and a reasonable local population in the area if not right next to it. This is where a location like Bodmin Road (or as it is today, Bodmin Parkway) would make sense as it's a decent sized station with justifiable facilities but few buildings nearby.

With a decent local population there's inevitably a need for some goods facilities, so at the very least some sidings are a must. A goods shed isn't such a necessity in my view, but somewhere to store goods wagons and shunt them are a must, even if it's only a couple of sidings and a headshunt.

Although engine sheds are nice space fillers and look pretty, if we're aiming for a veneer of realism, the chances that a small station in the sort of location we're starting to envisage would need its own depot would have been pretty slim. At best there would have been a stabling point where a small stud of locomotives could be watered and fuelled between duties, but in this context that would be fine: somewhere to showcase locomotives not on duty is perfect. Bewdley MPD on the Severn Valley Railway is a classic example of this and shows that you don't necessarily need a huge amount of space for a realistic motive power depot.

Some sort of branch line is important for me as it provides a bit more variety of traffic and also the opportunity for some remarshalling of freight trains a la Bodmin Road and Lostwithiel, as well as, perhaps, a single coach local passenger train.

Location, location

So, on this perfect layout we have station with some goods facilities and a small stabling point. When it comes to traffic variety is the spice of life, so in a perfect world we'd be able to legitimately justify a range of passenger and freight trains, preferably from more than one of the Big Four companies or British Railways regions. This is where we can really begin to finetune the setting for the layout. I've always loved the Great Western Railway and as *Hornby Magazine* has never done a GWR project layout before, the timing couldn't be better.

In my perfect layout, GWR trains would form a slight majority over those from somewhere else, and realistically that means that we have to choose between the London Midland & Scottish Railway (and predecessors) or the Southern Railway and its constituents. With all bar Bay Street Mk 2 and Ashland of *Hornby Magazine's* project layouts set in northern England, and with Hornby's recent 'T9' 4-4-0 and Kernow Model Rail Centre's '0298' 2-4-0WT available what could be more tantalising than a model railway set in North Cornwall, somewhere around Launceston where GWR and SR trains could run alongside each other and occasionally onto each other's metals.

The choice of the Launceston region is deliberate. The town itself was served by the GWR branch from Plymouth via Tavistock, while the SR ran through the town on the Halwill Junction-Wadebridge North Cornwall Railway. In the Second

World War the Railway Executive built a series of connections between the networks at Launceston and Lydford and St Budeaux to allow trains to run from the Far West should the Royal Albert Bridge at Saltash be put out of action. With the giant naval base of Devonport just next door to Brunel's structure this was a real possibility, so the move made sense from an operational perspective, but more importantly from our perspective, provides genuine historical justification for connecting GWR and SR metals.

The brief

This, then, is the reasoning theme for this year's *Hornby Magazine Yearbook* - a new layout which has to fit in a reasonable space, include a small station on a secondary Great Western Railway route in North Cornwall with a Southern Railway branch allow a mixture of rolling stock to operate without stretching the bounds of probability.

So, armed with the brief, it's over to *Hornby Magazine* Editor Mike Wild to translate ideas into action. In recognition of its location near, but not that near, to Launceston, the layout will be called St Stephens Road...

Planning
St Stephens Road

Layout planning is an exciting part of the development of a new project, but there are two methods – paper and real world. **MIKE WILD** explains how St Stephen's Road generated from an original brainwave through three very different arrangements.

This layout started out as a discussion. We had always planned to build a new layout for *Hornby Magazine Yearbook No. 4*, but until we started talking about it we didn't have any preconceived ideas apart from one – that it would be a BR Western Region theme project.

To date the *Hornby Magazine* team has built two Southern, two London Midland and one Eastern Region layout and some might say we've neglected the Western. That is until now. Initially we planned that the layout would use the now multi-purpose fiddle yards created for Berrybridge which were used this summer for *Hornby Magazine's* layout in a weekend challenge at Hornby Magazine LIVE! in Hartlepool.

After our first discussion about the new layout – which is called St Stephen's Road we set our selves a target scenic area of 8ft x 4ft (Plan 1). Initially we looked towards a simple continuous run layout and while this would have been potentially quick to build, it didn't really offer enough potential. It would however have allowed three coach trains and eight wagon goods workings (see trackplan) while also allowing continuous running of trains. Perhaps more importantly

ST STEPHENS ROAD, PLAN 1
(8ft x 4ft, 'OO' gauge, not to scale)

KEY

1. Fiddle yard
2. Back scene
3. Tunnel mouth
4. Level crossing
5. Road
6. Goods shed
7. Loading dock
8. Coal staithes
9. Coal office
10. Signalbox
11. Platform
12. Waiting room
13. Station builing
14. Houses
15. Church

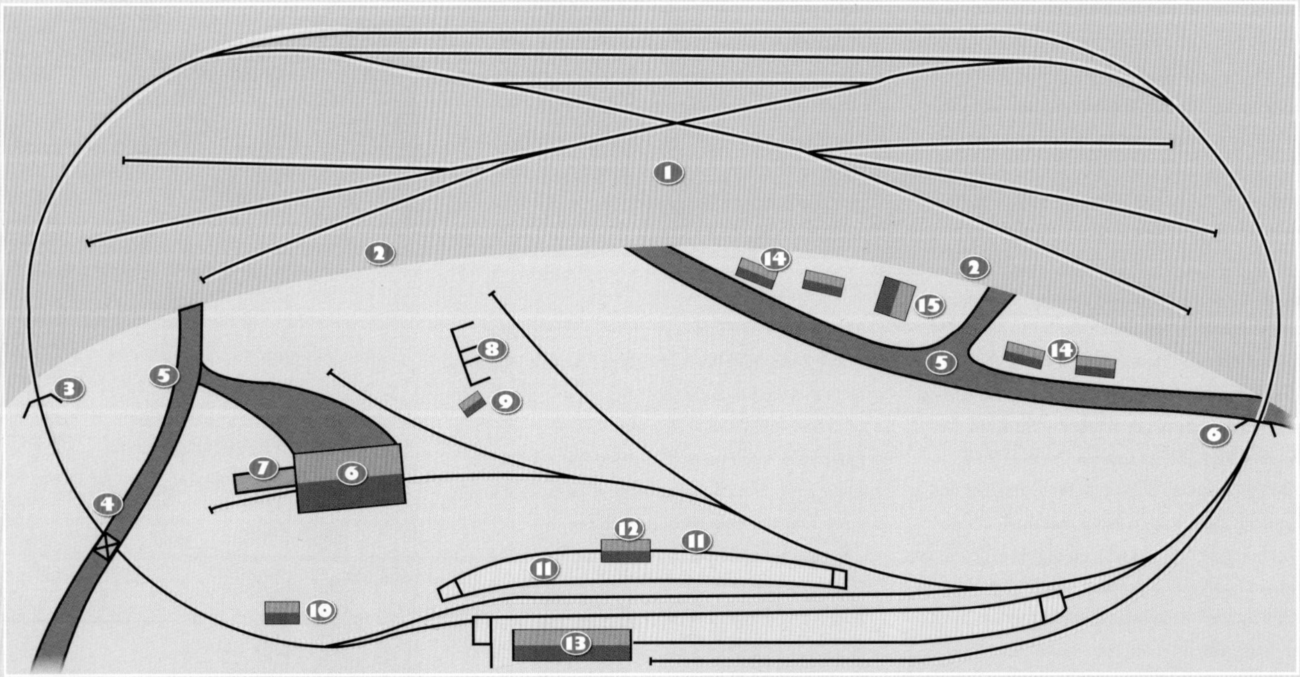

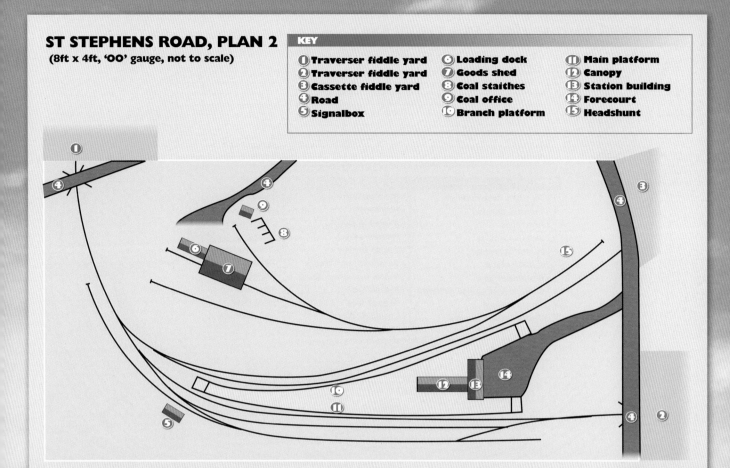

ST STEPHENS ROAD, PLAN 2
(8ft x 4ft, 'OO' gauge, not to scale)

KEY
1. Traverser fiddle yard
2. Traverser fiddle yard
3. Cassette fiddle yard
4. Road
5. Signalbox
6. Loading dock
7. Goods shed
8. Coal staithes
9. Coal office
10. Branch platform
11. Main platform
12. Canopy
13. Station building
14. Forecourt
15. Headshunt

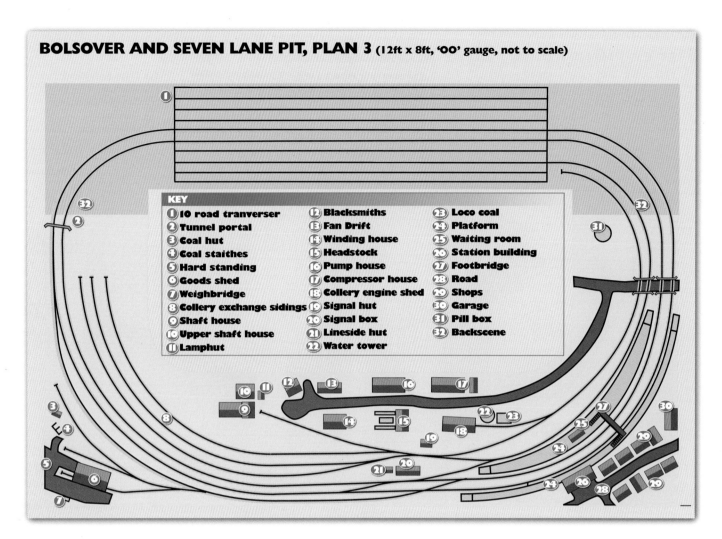

KEY

① 10 road tranverser	⑫ Blacksmiths	㉓ Loco coal
② Tunnel portal	⑬ Fan Drift	㉔ Platform
③ Coal hut	⑭ Winding house	㉕ Waiting room
④ Coal staithes	⑮ Headstock	㉖ Station building
⑤ Hard standing	⑯ Pump house	㉗ Footbridge
⑥ Goods shed	⑰ Compressor house	㉘ Road
⑦ Weighbridge	⑱ Collery engine shed	㉙ Shops
⑧ Collery exchange sidings	⑲ Signal hut	㉚ Garage
⑨ Shaft house	⑳ Signal box	㉛ Pill box
⑩ Upper shaft house	㉑ Lineside hut	㉜ Backscene
⑪ Lamphut	㉒ Water tower	

it would easily fit in an average spare bedroom being of modest size.

Version Two

So how did we decide to move on? Firstly we drew out a couple of schemes on paper and then, having built the baseboards, it brought us to our second design for St Stephen's Road. For this we used the same 8ft x 4ft footprint for the scenic area, but this time it was an end to end layout using the two fiddle yards from Berrybridge plus a requirement for a third storage yard to connect to the branch.

The total size of this project would have been 12ft x 8ft (Plan 2) which would have potential to be housed in either a garage or shed location or, with management permission, a large spare bedroom.

This design reached the point where all the track was laid, but then we realised that it was physically floored in terms of our planned operation. We had our suspicions that it would be difficult working with 4ft wide baseboards, but equally we liked the opportunity for a wide space on which to build the layout. It featured a three road goods yard, a complex junction formed from

Peco large radius curved points and an impressive station space with the main line running through one platform face and the branch on the opposite side forming a triangular station. However, the design – which featured two goods loops to the front of the plan – meant that we would have been unable to uncouple locomotives using our preferred methods.

This was a shame as the concept looked superb, even with just the track laid on the bare baseboards, but something had to give. The question now turned to how best to utilise the four 4ft x 2ft baseboards which formed St Stephens Road in its current form as we didn't want to start from scratch with wood work, especially with the deadline approaching for the layout.

Version Three

A series of decisions then followed to come up with the final concept for St Stephens Road. Using the four 4ft x 2ft baseboards which had already been built for the layout we rearranged them in an 'L' shape offering an 8ft long scenic area on one side and a 10ft scenic area on the return of the 'L'. This offered a lot of potential and also saw further

redesigning of the trackplan to fit the space.

The downside of the final version is that its total footprint (including fiddle yards) is 12ft x 14ft, but it offers a lot of operational potential within that space with the main line format remaining virtually unchanged, but with drastic alterations to the branch line and goods yard arrangement. These changes though have made the layout simple to operate and a pleasure to look at as the sweeping curves of the trackplan have a natural feel to them.

Plan 4 shows the final arrangement for St Stephen's Road.

Black, green and blue

Rolling stock is an important consideration in any layout project. Some prefer a free for all operating whatever stock they fancy and this is more than plausible. After all, it is your layout and you can run what you want on it.

For St Stephens Road we wanted to stick with a Western Region theme, but equally have some ability to vary the exact period which operates on it. Our primary period would be the 1955-1965 steam-diesel transition era, but with our editor's soft spot for Western Region diesel hydraulics and the impending release of Dapol's Class 22 we also wanted to be able to run the layout purely with diesel traction in the green era from 1960-1968.

As a third option we also wanted the layout to be able to accommodate early BR blue diesels and including the early TOPS numbering scheme introduced in 1971. For the are in question this wouldn't be too difficult. Signalling and infrastructure on this type of line barely changed during the early 1970s so we felt that it was quite feasible to simply change over the rolling stock and operate the layout in a totally different guise.

When planning a layout it is always worth considering what types and lengths of train will operate on it. For example, there is no point building a branch line if you really want to be able to run express trains and with a different track arrangement in a 12ft x 8ft area (Plan 3) it is perfectly feasible to create a main line atmosphere. The layout shown in Plan 3 is *Hornby Magazine's* latest exhibition layout Bolsover which was sponsored by Hornby and featured in supplements with HM45 and HM46.

Although it has been designed as an Eastern Region layout, the plan proves that a main line scene in 12ft x 8ft is possible and through the traverser fiddle yard design (which has no points and maximises train lengths) it allows for 20 wagon goods trains and six or seven coach trains depending on vehicle lengths.

For St Stephen's Road our train lengths were pre-determined by the use of Berrybridge's fiddle yards. These allow for three coach trains with a tender engine or eight wagons goods with a brake van and locomotive added on top. In total the four fiddle yards can hold 18 trains when full, allowing one through and one DMU line free on one turntable so that trains have a space to arrive at the alternative end.

Planned

St Stephen's Road has been a, perhaps, slightly awkward layout to design and, in fact, has become much larger than we had originally anticipated. However, its final track layout and design offers a strong range of operation coupled with a good running length so the trains can be seen in both the station and countryside while having an opportunity to stretch their legs.

The twin routes - with one through line for the Western Region and one for the Southern Region - give it a different twist and should also allow a continuous flow of trains at exhibitions. This latter point is always important to us as we feel we should put on a show at an exhibition so we need to be able to provide a good flow of trains.
In this Yearbook we will follow construction of this new layout.

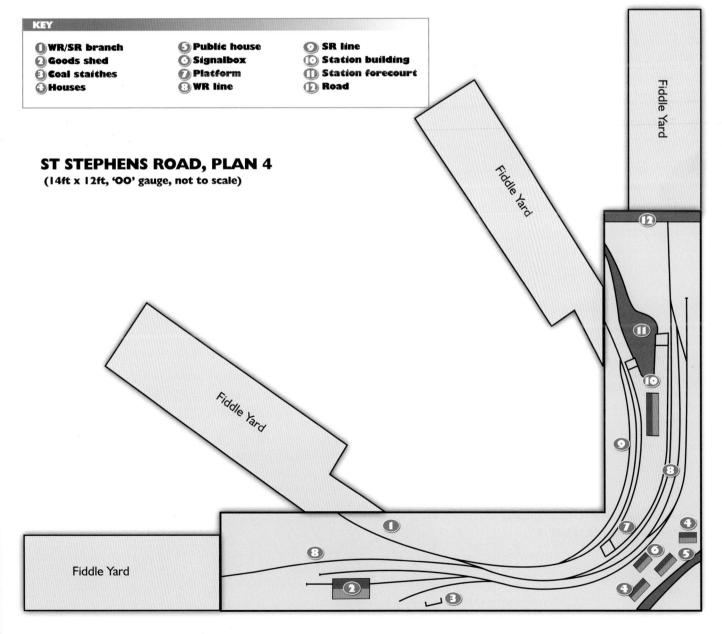

KEY

1. WR/SR branch
2. Goods shed
3. Coal staithes
4. Houses
5. Public house
6. Signalbox
7. Platform
8. WR line
9. SR line
10. Station building
11. Station forecourt
12. Road

ST STEPHENS ROAD, PLAN 4
(14ft x 12ft, 'OO' gauge, not to scale)

The unsung heroes
of the steam railway

Always in the background and invariably overshadowed by larger and more glamorous types, the 0-6-0 was by far the most important steam locomotive of all. **Andrew Roden** explains why every steam era modeller should consider expanding their fleet.

NUMBERS OF 0-6-0 LOCOMOTIVES BY COMPANY

	1947	1955	1960	1965
GWR	183	122	82	0
LMS	2180	1596	994	11
SR	325	246	169	3
LNER	1698	1311	693	90
Total	4386	3275	1938	104

Percentages of 0-6-0s in tender locomotive fleets, 31/12/47

GWR	12.88
LMS	39.13
SR	28.26
LNER	39.03

Nothing epitomises steam age Britain better than an 0-6-0 tender locomotive. For 140 years from their inception in 1827 until the last were withdrawn in 1967 they hauled freight and passengers over the length and breadth of Britain. They did it efficiently and without fuss - yet are barely represented on most model railways.

Asked to describe the typical British steam locomotive of the 20th century, most of us would probably envisage a mixed traffic 4-6-0 with outside cylinders, Walschaerts valve gear and driving wheels of around 6ft diameter. And this plays out on countless layouts, which have a station, an engine shed, a goods shed and a few domestic buildings. A small tank engine will shunt the yard while mixed traffic 4-6-0s tackle the bulk of the passenger service. Freight will be handled by a few 2-8-0s or 2-10-0s, and a big 4-6-0 or 4-6-2 will haul the most prestigious

expresses.

In fact, and as the panels show, to an astonishing degree, on all bar the Great Western, 0-6-0s were the most common or second most common type of locomotive. The GWR only escapes that fact because it used 0-6-0PTs on duties the other railways rostered a tender locomotive for.

The figures are truly astounding. In 1947, the last year of the 'Big Four', of the total stock of 12,491 tender locomotives, 4,386 were 0-6-0s - 35% of the total tender locomotive fleet. The next most common type, the 4-6-0, came a long way behind, with 2,503 examples or 20% of the total. This dominance, amazingly, continued until the end of 1958, and it wasn't until 1962 that the number of 0-6-0s fell below 1,000. Unless you model the Great Western, if yours is a steam layout, you need more 0-6-0s than 2-6-0s and 4-6-0s. For the London Midland and Scottish and London and North Eastern Railways, to be

LYR '2F' 52619 approaches Farington with shed empties from Preston to Bamfurlong in April 1951.

LNER 'J38' 0-6-0 65923 climbs away from Cameron Bridge with a Methil Docks to Thornton goods in March 1958. W Verden Anderson/ Rail Archive Stephenson.

truly representative, around four out of every 10 of your steam locomotives should be 0-6-0s.

The problem modellers face is the sheer multiplicity of types. Even at nationalisation, when one might imagine that more modern designs had displaced them, there were some striking anachronisms roaming the rails. The oldest design in revenue earning service, as far as one can tell, was the former

Midland Railway double-framed '2F', exemplified by 58110, which was withdrawn in 1951 aged 81 and whose design goes back to the 1860s. However, the famous London and North Western Railway 'Coal Engines' were more representative of the veterans, with 46 in traffic at nationalisation. There were other Victorian 0-6-0s which lasted into British Railways service too, such as the Great

Western Railway's 'Dean Goods' of 1883, the former Caledonian Railway '2F' Barton Wright Class 25 of 1876, the North Eastern Railway's 'J21s' of 1886 and the Adams '0395s' of 1881.

Far more representative were the '2251s' of the GWR, the ex-South Eastern and Chatham Railway 'Cs' of the Southern Railway, the hundreds of '3Fs' and '4Fs' of the London Midland & Scottish Railway,

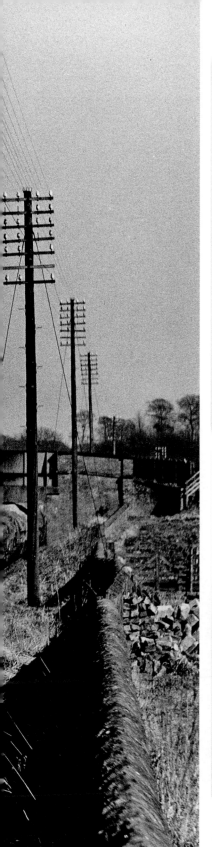

READY-TO-RUN 0-6-0 MODELS

'OO' gauge

Company	Class	Liveries	Manufacturer
GWR	'2251'	GWR Green, BR black	Bachmann
GWR	'Dean Goods'	GWR green	Hornby*
SR	'700'	BR black	OO Works*
SR	'C'	SECR Green, SR Black, BR black	Bachmann***
SR	'Q1'	SR/BR black	Hornby
LMS	'2F'	BR black	OO Works
LMS	'3F'	LMS/BR black	Bachmann**
LMS	'4F'	LMS/BR black	Hornby**
LNER	'J39'	LNER/BR black	Bachmann*

*Past product - availability may be limited
**Due late 2011
***Due 2012

'N' gauge

Company	Class	Liveries	Manufacturer
GWR	'2251'	GWR green/BR black	Peco
LMS	'4F'	BR black	Bachmann
LNER	'J39'	LNER/BR black	Bachmann*

*Due 2012

and the LNER's 'J39s'. For those who model any period from the 1930s to the late 1950s and beyond in some cases, these classes are amongst the most important of all. Thankfully they will soon all be available in 'OO' gauge.

In the background
It is hard to remember now just how prevalent the 0-6-0s were until the end of the 1950s. Most of them

Above: Former GER 'J15' 65477 pilots 'D16/3' 4-4-0 62610 with the 2pm Cambridge-Newmarket as it heads away from Cambridge on May 6 1957. David Hepburne-Scott/Rail Archive Stephenson.

Left: GWR '2251' 0-6-0 2227 passes Fochrhiw with a train of empty coke wagons on August 14 1957. Bob Tuck/Rail Archive Stephenson.

Fowler '4F' 44134 passes Disley South Junction with an up freight on July 4 1959. Kenneth Field/Rail Archive Stephenson.

POPULAR 0-6-0 CHARACTERISTICS

Class	'2251'	'C'	'J39'	'4F'
Company	GWR	SECR/SR	LNER	MR/SDJR/LMS
Designer	Collett	Wainwright	Gresley	Fowler
Built	1930-48	1900-08	1926-41	1911-22, 1924-40
Number in traffic, 31/12/47	118 (+2 in 1948)	108	289	772
Power classification	3MT	3F (2F post1953)	4F (5F post 1953)	4F
Wheel diameter	5ft 2in	5ft 2in	5ft 2in	5ft 3in
Tractive effort	20,155lb	19,520lb	25,665lb	24,555lb
Locomotive weight	43t 8cwt	43t 16cwt	57t 17cwt	48t 15cwt
Tender weight	36t 5cwt	38t 5cwt	44t 4cwt	41t 4cwt

plodded away in the background on slow goods trains day in, day out, performing the unglamorous and mundane tasks which made the railways money.

They were in a very real sense, part of the railway scenery that went as unremarked as the smoke that issued from their chimneys, yet they were a peculiarly British institution. From the first, Timothy Hackworth's *Royal George* for the Stockton and Darlington Railway in 1827, they developed via outside framed designs to what became the definitive template in the 1880s. From then on, most 0-6-0s had driving wheels of between 4ft 6in and 5ft 8in diameter, with cylinders ranging from 17in x 24in on the smaller classes to 19in x 26in, and even in some cases 20in diameter. Tractive efforts tended to be around 20,000lbs or less, but as Gresley's impressive 'J39s' showed, it could be over 25,000lbs, and for Bulleid's striking 'Q1s', over 30,000lb. The valve gear was almost always inside, and most commonly of Stephenson link motion type.

Developments were incremental from the 1880s. Power gradually increased, though by the early 1900s larger 0-8-0 and 2-6-0 types were entering traffic and the advent of superheating in the 1910s allowed a modest rise in power and efficiency, though how often their duties called on superheating is questionable for many classes. As a format the 0-6-0 was arguably outmoded even by the time of grouping in 1923 but its elemental simplicity and versatility persuaded all of the 'Big Four' railways to build more. The pick of the bunch were

The Southern Railway's CME Oliver Bulleid produced the most powerful 0-6-0 design in the 'Q1'. On September 13 1964 'Q1' 0-6-0 33009 approaches Woking on the line from Guildford with a permanent way train. **Brian Stephenson.**

probably the '2251s' of the GWR, the LNER's 'J39s' and Bulleid's astounding 'Q1s' of the SR. The GWR's answer was designed specifically for mixed traffic duties and became known as 'Baby Castles' by their crews thanks to their eager acceleration and good turn of speed. By contrast, Bulleid's 'Q1' was firmly a freight design, with the power of a 'Black Five'.

Versatility

The duties of the 0-6-0s were as varied as their myriad forms. While the older and lower powered classes eked out their existence hauling short pick-up goods trains which

more powerful locomotives would be wasted on, others were regulars on passenger trains. Indeed, the LMS '4Fs' were widely used on these duties as they had an excellent turn of speed and were only classified as freight locomotives after nationalisation. The typical 0-6-0 might have been humble but it was also versatile enough for the operating conditions of the time - and in truth, it wasn't worth railways spending the money on more advanced designs given the miniscule gains from doing so.

Even on our GWR project layout St Stephens Road, we really ought to have at least one 0-6-0 to be representative - and what could look prettier on a secondary route than a '2251' sprinting away from the station with a short passenger train as they did so often on the old Didcot, Newbury and Southampton? For other regions the case for having a strong fleet of 0-6-0s is compelling too. With Bachmann's forthcoming '3F' and Hornby's '4F' in 'OO' scale together with a reasonable range of counterparts from other regions, the value of these unsung heroes is finally being recognised.

From a modelling perspective their relatively small size and wide range of workloads makes them vastly easier to justify than a big 'Pacific' and much more practical on small layout too.

Hardly any steam era standard gauge layout can afford to be without a decent stud of these overlooked but crucial locomotives: they may lack glamour but they make up for it in sheer utility.

Digital developments

2011 witnessed a range of impressive and important developments for Digital Command Control. Chief among these is Hornby's new RailMaster software. **Mike Wild** explains why and details the latest innovations in model railway technology. *Photography, Mike Wild.*

DCC control is becoming increasingly popular with exhibition layouts. The North Fylde Model Railway Club has introduced DCC on its January 1968 depot layout offering greater interest to the operators with sound fitted motive power.

J ust when it seems like it has all gone quiet, something comes out of the woodwork and revolutionises Digital model railway operation. Since the introduction of Digital Command Control there has been a sticking point in the control of points and signals – not least because many systems rely on a degree of operator knowledge and memory in order to make the most of this flexible system.

However, that all changed in June this year when Hornby launched its promised RailMaster computer control system which works hand in hand with its Elite DCC controller.

If you have been around DCC you will know that computer control is nothing new. However, it has never before been produced on a level where literally anyone with a laptop or desktop computer could harness its capabilities.

Unlike its competitors RailMaster is what most would describe as a budget system, but just because it has a lower priced doesn't mean its inferior – in fact

quite the opposite. Sofisticated and intuitive are two of the best words to describe this new software which connects with the Elite through a USB cable to take control of locomotives and their functions, points and accessories.

RailMaster has been developed by a third party for Hornby and currently retails for just £60 while the Elite has a price point of £199. So, for a couple of pence under £260 you can have a fully operational computer controlled model railway system and one which can be used with any computer operating system from Windows 98 to the latest Windows 7.

What RailMaster does

In simple terms RailMaster becomes the controller for a railway. Customised trackplans can be drawn using the simple to operate Matrix planning section and locomotives can be listed into the software using their unique DCC addresses – just as you would with a DCC controller.

On starting the programme RailMaster provides a track diagram with provision for point operation, signals and more meaning that, in effect, it becomes a virtual control panel similar to what many modellers produce using conventional analogue control. The Elite, in effect, becomes a black box, but equally the driving force of the

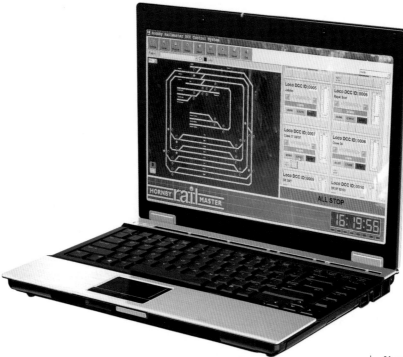

system as all signals from RailMaster are transferred through the Elite to operate the railway.

However, there is much more to this new software than simply controlling trains. It can read and write CV values through a programming track connected to the Elite, it can store thousands of locomotives and it can also provide preset speed settings for shunting and cruising. Moreover route selection is all part of its abilities and, perhaps its most impressive component, the ability to

automate either part or a whole layout system.

Hornby Magazine was involved in beta testing RailMaster before its launch and from our experience at exhibitions we have found it to be highly stable and simple to operate . Locomotive sound and light functions can be controlled at the click of a mouse and it provides all of what you get from a cab control panel, but with a more modern, fresh feeling.

There is more to come too, but that, as they say, is another story.

Above: Hornby's RailMaster has been a great innovation for those looking for a simple, robust and stable computer control system for a model railway. It connects to the Hornby Elite DCC controller through a USB cable to operate a layout.

Below: This year has seen ESU introduce a new version of its highly popular LokSound decoder – V4.0. This 21-pin decoder features a range of upgrades. This is a Bachmann 'O4' with a Howes Models sound chip using the LokSound V4.0 installed in the tender.

Decoder upgrades

However, it isn't just Hornby which is making progress with DCC. This year three manufacturers have stepped up to provide new locomotive decoders to assist modellers in their quest for excellence.

The ESU LokSound decoders are well established with those making use of sound fitted locomotives, but following the Nurnberg exhibition in Germany the manufacturer introduced its new v4.0 LokSound decoder. This 21-pin locomotive decoder has all the capabilities of its predecessor and more to boot. These include improved motor control with ESU's fifth generation of motor management, the ability to add a power peak pack which acts as a 'stay alive' system should a locomotive run over dirty track and the ability to have up to eight independent sound channels running at the same time from each decoder.

Having tested two of the LokSound v4.0 decoders from Howes Models – featuring the sounds of a Robinson 'O4' and Riddles 'Britannia' – we found all of the manufacturers statements to be true. Slow speed control was first rate and throughout the speed range and we also noticed an increased quality to the sounds produced through the supplied 23mm speaker.

Similarly Zimo has introduced its MX645 sound decoder which is pre wired for a capacitor to be connected to it to provide a 'stay alive' feature. This decoder offers a broad range of functions which allow it to control such features as locomotive lights and, as illustrated by Paul Chetter's features in *Hornby Magazine*, smoke generators. For the latter the Zimo MX645 has a high output available – necessary to power a smoke generator on DCC – which makes this the first choice sound and function decoder for those wishing to add working smoke to steam locomotives. Also worth noting is that the Zimo decoder, as with the LokSound sound decoder, can be loaded with custom sounds opening up a new range of possibilities.

Australian manufacturer DCC Concepts began launching its new range of DCC locomotive decoders in July with the arrival of both its four function and two function decoders. Both are available either with or without a 'stay alive' capacitor allowing smoother operation of locomotives as small power outages will no longer be noticed by the decoder or operator alike. Further versions including smaller sized decoders with differing outputs are also coming from DCC Concepts.

Accessory decoders have also been introduced for DCC Concepts Cobalt slow action point motors offering further creativity to DCC layout builders.

Below: DCC Concepts has begun introducing its new range of decoders including two and four function decoders with 'stay alive' capacitors. These neat installations are a boon to shunting locomotives under digital control as well as main line engines.

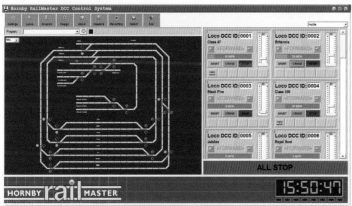

Locomotives

Digital is now a major part of ready-to-run locomotives. Hornby has embraced digital to the full and now offers the majority of its 'OO' gauge range – where a decoder socket is provided – both with and without a factory installed decoder.

Bachmann is continuing its push with DCC in 2011 by producing new chassis for its Gresley 'A4', Thompson 'B1' and Gresley 'V2' with an 8-pin decoder socket to replace the previous split chassis design.

Furthermore Bachmann has also embraced 21-pin decoders and when

brand new locomotives are produced these are equipped with this interface, except for a few steam locomotives which make use of existing tender toolings.

The range of ready-to-run sound fitted locomotives is also increasing with Hornby adding the Stanier 'Princess Royal' 4-6-2 to its DCC sound range to join the 'Black Five', 'A4', 'Schools' and 'Castle' from the steam range. Bachmann is adding DCC sound to its 'Patriot' 4-6-0, 'Super D' 0-8-0 and 'A1' 4-6-2 with the latter two locomotives due for release before the end of 2011.

Digital has always been a growing sector of model railways, but in 2011 it has benefitted from a range of new upgrades. These are expanding its possibilities as well as making its more accessible, user friendly and attractive.

Above: The potential of digital control in 'N' gauge is growing as the vast majority of new production locomotives now feature a 6-pin DCC decoder socket built into the chassis. A Bachmann 'Peak' with hard wired decoder and a Dapol 'Britannia' with a 6-pin plug in decoder pass on *Hornby Magazine's* Hettle layout which also uses Hornby RailMaster to control the trains.

Left: RailMaster can control locomotives, sound functions, points, signals and more. Using the Design facility for the programme any trackplan can be drawn for operation with the software. This is the finished and operational plan for Hettle.

St Stephens Road
– baseboards and trackwork

With a plan set it's time to turn to the baseboards and trackwork for our project layout. **Mike Wild** describes how the baseboards developed and how the track was laid. *Photography, Mike Wild.*

Building baseboards is sometimes seen as a difficult aspect of model railway construction, but it certainly doesn't have to be. For *Hornby Magazine's* layouts we use a tried and tested method which results in a strong, light weight and rigid base on which to build a railway.

The bare bones of these are 9mm plywood sheet timber and 20mm x 70mm planed timber for the frame work. You don't have to be an expert with a saw to build a baseboard, although a handful of tools are essential for home construction. As a minimum you will need a screwdriver, electric if you prefer, a tennon saw or an electric jigsaw and that's about it. A workbench is handy, but for a more cost effective option you can buy saw horses which provide a simple and convenient workstation which can be stored just as easily.

One area to consider when it comes to baseboard construction is the purpose of the layout. Will it be a permanent fixture or does it need to be portable – either for exhibition purposes or simply for storage? We use 9mm plywood for our baseboard surfaces and this can be bought in 8ft x 4ft, 6ft x 2ft and 4ft x 2ft sheets from most DIY outlets. Equally timber merchants and some DIY stores offer a cutting service for sheet timber which, while adding a couple of pounds to the cost of the wood, will save a lot of time when it comes to the construction process.

An important factor to consider when purchasing timber is how it has been stored. Timber stored on end will warp out of shape before it is purchased and this especially prevalent in sheet timber. Timber merchants by their nature tend to store sheet timber flat which keeps it straight and true. However, planed timber, in our experience, is invariably stored upright so it is worth being selective to find the best quality in terms of straightness available at the time of purchase.

St Stephens' foundation

Our method for baseboard construction follows a well rehearsed routine. Knowing that we wanted to work with 4ft x 2ft baseboards simplified matters greatly as the 9mm plywood we used was available pre-cut from a local outlet to those measurements – give or take a couple of millimetres.

Essentially this meant that all we had to

A 'Warship' hydraulic rubs shoulders with a 'Hymek' on the Western Region side of St Stephens Road. In the background an 'N' 2-6-0 stands in the loop on the Southern Region side of the station.

Above: A 'Hymek' ambles along the Western Region branch to St Stephens Road passing the site of the goods yard.

Right: The new arrangement for St Stephens Road's baseboards offers much greater potential and a longer running line. The trackplan also features two separate branch line routes.

do was construct a framework for each baseboard to support the top sheets – without a frame the thin ply wouldn't be strong enough to support train or accommodate any of the electrics.

We prefer to cut all of our timber to length for each baseboard in one go, rather than chopping and changing between actions. This results in a form of mini production line as each board can then be assembled by fixing the sides, ends and cross braces in place (in that order) with wood screws (see diagram).

With the four 4ft x 2ft baseboards prepared we needed a method of supporting them. This came in the form of 3ft 6in high trestles which were built to suit the baseboards. These are formed of four lengths of 20mm x 70mm timber all 3ft 6in long and four lengths of the same timber 2ft long. The longer lengths were fixed 25mm in from each end of the 2ft lengths so that the baseboard frame could sit over the top of the trestle – the longer length protruding above the top bar by 60mm.

With all the baseboards and trestles construction the four 4ft x 2ft boards were laid out to create an 8ft x 4ft layout initially. On this we drew out two different trackplans before commencing construction of the trackwork. However,

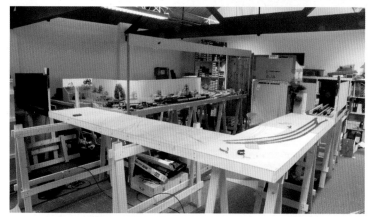

after laying out our proposed trackplan – see the feature on pages 12-17 – we realised despite the idea being attractive in terms of operation and size by offering a total of 12ft x 8ft including the fiddle yards, that what we had proposed simply wouldn't work operationally.

The problem came in access. Our crew wouldn't be able to reach to the front goods loops to uncouple locomotives or wagons and none of the currently available automatic uncouplers for tension lock couplings really suited what we wanted – particularly as uncoupling positions would have to be pre-determined. So with the design inoperable it was back to the drawing board.

Thanks to the style of baseboard we used the four 4ft x 2ft sections were separated out again after removing the majority of the track. We wanted to retain the arrangement of the goods loops and station approach, albeit with a couple of amendments, so the main junctions were left in place for the rearrangement process.

To create the final baseboard arrangement for St Stephens Road we decided upon an 'L' shape arrangement as show in the feature on pages 12-17. This resulted in a fully operable layout with manual uncoupling which would allowing shunting to take place throughout the station and goods yard area.

STEP 1 - Start by marking up the 8ft lengths of 70mm x 20mm timber to create the framework to support the plywood top. Each board for this layout required two 1,200mm lengths and four 570mm long to match the overall size of the board. Measure twice with a tape measure then use a square to mark the cut line.

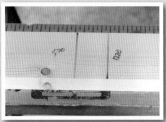

STEP 2: Once the cut lines are marked make a note next to each one to show the length of the finished timber. This makes it easy to identify which length you are looking at, particularly if a baseboard requires different length frame pieces.

STEP 3: With all the timber lengths marked up, cutting begins. You can do this with a hand saw such as a tenon saw and mitre block to create 90 degree cuts or, as in our case, use a chop saw. Be careful when using a chop saw as the blades are sharp and they spin very fast.

STEP 4: Once all the timber is cut you will end up with something like this. The long lengths match the longest side of the baseboard while the short lengths, which fit inside the outer long pieces, are 36mm shorter than the baseboard top to take into account the 18mm width of the outer timbers. At the bottom is the stack of precut 1,200mm x 600mm plywood sheets.

STEP 5: Assembly begins with a mock-up of the timber framework on the first of the baseboard tops. This ensures everything will fit together as planned. Once happy with this, move onto the next step.

STEP 6: Start by fixing the outer long lengths to the baseboard top. We use easy drive wood screws and a drill driver to screw these into the timber. Start with one screw at each end, then one in the centre (ensuring that the timber is in line with the baseboard top, then add screws every 6in between the first three screws.

STEP 7: With both sides of the frame in place, stretchers can be added to support the centre of the baseboard and keep it rigid. Use a square to set these straight against the frame sides then screw through the side into the stretcher to support it in place. Once this is done turn the baseboard over and mark a line for the location of the stretcher on the baseboard top. Add screws every 6in along this line.

STEP 8: Finally the ends can be added to the framework. Carefully place these between the sides and secure in place with screws from above and through the ends of the sides. For the latter it may be necessary to make a pilot hole to avoid splitting the timber when the screw is driven home. This process is then repeated for all subsequent baseboards.

STEP 9: Next on the list is a set of supports for the layout. We built our own trestles which consist of four lengths of 69mm x 18mm timber 1,000mm long and four lengths of 600mm long timber. Set the 1,000mm lengths 25mm in from the ends of the 600mm lengths to create a support point for the baseboard frames.

STEP 10: Each trestle is formed of two identical halves. These are joined at the top by butt hinges, using screws to secure these in place and allowing the trestle to be folded away when not in use.

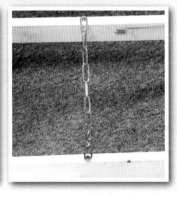

STEP 11: A trestle needs a method to stop the legs simply falling away from one another. To do this we used metal chain cut into 12-link lengths. This is then secured to the lowered trestle stretcher with wood screws.

STEP 12: With all of the timber work complete for the baseboards, assembly is next. Start by placing two baseboards on their respective trestles and clamp them together with a pair of G-clamps. We used M6 (6mm diameter) coach bolts to join the baseboards together, so a 6mm wood drill was used to create two holes through the baseboard frame. Before drilling ensure that the tops of the two baseboards meet perfectly level.

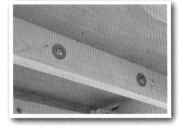

STEP 13: Coach bolts can then be inserted into the holes with a washer between the head and the timber to spread the load. These are 30mm washers.

STEP 14: Finally secure each coach bolt, and in turn baseboard frame, together with wing nuts.

Trestles are used to support the baseboards for this project. These can be arranged in piggyback fashion to allow each board, apart from the first to be erected, to be supported by one trestle.

The arrangement also offers a much longer run for the trains. One side of the scenic section is 10ft long and features the main Western Region branch which is then joined by the joint Western/Southern Region line which also serves as a branch to a china clay dry. On the opposite side of the Western Region route is a goods yard which serves local businesses and farms.

As the line approaches the station it runs alongside the Southern Region route with the two then running into opposite sides of the platform. The Southern side has a single platform face, but includes a loop for passing goods. The Western side, which also provides access to the goods yard, has a single platform face and two goods loops, the outer of which accesses the goods yard and also acts as an extended headshunt as required.

Laying the track

Although conventional logic generally says that a plan should be drawn out on paper before construction begins, in some cases it can be easier to work the opposite way round. St Stephens Road developed on the baseboards. We

already had a selection of points available from the first version – all from Peco's code 75 range and including medium and curved radius points together with a box of flexible track to match - and all but one of these has been used in the new arrangement.

Initially the track was laid out loose on the baseboards to get a picture of how it might look. With a few tweaks track laying then began from the station approach on the shorter viewing side of the 'L' by fixing the three points leading into the Western Region goods loops in place on top of a 1/16in cork sheet.

At the time of laying each point the holes for the point motor and frog polarity wires were drilled before it was fixed in place. For point motors we use a 10mm drill and for the polarity wires a 2mm drill both of which provide plenty of clearance for their respective purposes.

All of the code 75 track components

require rail joiners to be fitted and where necessary insulated joiners were fitted to suit the electrical plan for the layout – see feature on pages 36-39 for full details of the electrics for this project. Another important part of the track laying stage, particular with St Stephens being an exhibition layout, was to install copper clad sleepers at the baseboard joins by pinning them to the baseboards and soldering the rails to them to make a secure and robust joint between each baseboard.

With all the track laid basic wiring was installed to allow the layout to be tested before any further progress took place. While it might be seen as playing trains, this is always an important part of any layout project – if it doesn't work at this stage it is much easier to correct any problems.

The step by step guides which this feature outline the main principles of baseboard construction and trackwork.

STEP-BY-STEP LAYING THE TRACK FOR ST STEPHENS ROAD

STEP 1: The first stage in laying the track is to begin mocking up the track arrangement. We find it helps to make sense of the trackwork by placing trains in different locations during this process to assess how the railway will look.

STEP 2: Track laying begins at one of the fiddle yard entrances by installing the pointwork. This acts as a datum for the rest of the layout's track.

STEP 3: At the same time as the track is being laid the holes for the point motor and frog polarity wires are drilled. A 10mm hole provides adequate space for the point motor operating rod and a 2mm hole provides space for the frog polarity wire to be inserted through the board. These positions are marked on the baseboard with the point in place.

A '57XX' 0-6-0PT draws a china clay train into the middle goods loop at the future site of the station. The layout is very much under construction.

STEP 6: As this is a portable layout the baseboards for the scenic section separate into four pieces. To allow the track to separate copper clad strips are pinned to the baseboard and soldered to the rails - a groove being made in the copper strip between the two rails to stop short circuits. A cutting disc in a mini drill is the perfect tool for this job.

STEP 4: With all the track laid the next important addition are the dropper wires for electrical connections - see Electrics section on pages 36-41 for the full diagram. Two different coloured wires are soldered to each rail as required to provide power to the layout. These will in turn be fed into the control panel and through switches.

STEP 5: Wires - seven strand multi-core wire in this case - can be fed through 1mm holes in the baseboard to conceal their appearance.

STEP 7: The final stage in the track laying process is to paint the rails and sleepers for a weathered look. To do this we cover the point blades with strips of masking tape then spray paint the entire track with Railmatch frame dirt. The rail tops can then be cleaned with a track rubber to restore operation.

Powering
St Stephens

Every model railway needs electrical circuits to make it work, but despite many seeing this as a difficult exercise it doesn't have to be. **Mike Wild** explains how St Stephens Road has been wired for analogue control. *Photography, Mike Wild.*

I f I had to pick out three words which strike fear into railway modellers they would be, in no particular order, weathering, electrics and baseboards. Of these three electrics always seem to be a common source of difficulties, but this part of model railway construction only has to be complex if you make it so.

For St Stephens Road we are going back to analogue control. This means more wiring underneath the layout and also building a control panel with a mimic diagram. This diagram which is drawn onto a wood panel represents the trackplan of the layout, but with switches and point control studs where appropriate. This is the most common form of control panel and puts the layout in a simple order for operation.

The vast majority of model railway electrics are in fact quite simple. The circuits themselves are repetition of the same basic feeds – in short a positive

and a negative power supply fed from a transformer through a controller. Where it appears to become complex is in the number of wires required, but this comes down to working methodically, labeling and – if you wish – making notes.

Splitting up the power

At the very first stage of track laying it is important to decide where insulated rail joiners will be placed and how the layout will be broken up electrically. For St Stephens we have used live frog points which means that each time we create a passing loop it must have both rails broken at some point along it for the electrical side to work correctly.

This sounds difficult, but in reality it is very simple. For permanent home based layouts insulated rail joiners, which are plastic rather than metal, are the perfect tool for the job, but when it comes to a portable layout like St Stephens it is possible to take advantage of the baseboard breaks where the tracks have to be cut for portability. This means there are only a handful of insulated rail joiners installed on this layout with the rest of the section breaks being created by the baseboard joins – see Figure 1.

With the section breaks planned out we now need wiring connections to make the layout work. With analogue control this means switches and St Stephens Road has eight section switches that control different parts of the layout.

Throughout this layout we have used Double Pole Double Throw (DPDT) switches which have two paired input connections and a single paired output with two wires to each side of the switch and two leaving the centre to connect to the track. This means that with two controllers connected to the layout either one of these can be used to control a train on any part of the layout.

In its basic form the layout is split into two operator areas – one for the Western Region through route and one for the Southern Region route. However, should the Southern Region operator wish to bring a freight from the Southern line onto the Western line, a simple change of a couple of switches allow them to do so without having to change controllers – the Southern controller being used throughout. Similarly if the Western Region operator is busy running through trains and the

Main image: A 'Hymek' leads a van train through St Stephens Road. The Southern and Western Region routes can be controlled independently through the DPDT swtiches on the control panel.

Top left: The control panel starts as a plain piece of hardboard cut to the size required for the control panel. 6mm holes are drilled for the DPDT switches and 2.5mm holes for the point control studs.

Below left: The studs are then pressed through the previously drilled holes so that wiring connections can be added to the rear.

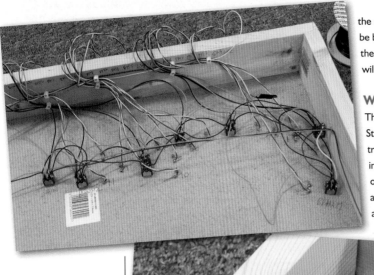

Above: Inside the control panel the wiring appears to be a maze. However, each pair of wires is the repetition of the same simple circuit.

Right: A Gaugemaster CDU provides a strong current to the point motors and ensures they change reliably.

Below: Keeping wiring neat makes a big difference, particularly when it comes to fault finding. These wires are held in place with staples.

the more flexibility which can be built into the control panel the more enjoyable the layout will be.

Wiring connections

The electrical installations for St Stephens started at the track laying stage as outlined in the feature on pages 30-35 of this book. This involved adding wire droppers at all the points where an

Southern operator fancies a change of scene, by changing over the DPDT switch for the goods yard the Southern operator can take control of this area of the layout independently of the rest of it.

This all comes down to planning and a vision of how a layout will work once built, but for the analogue layout builder

electrical connection will be needed either through a switch or to transfer power between two baseboards.

An important point to remember at this stage is to cut all wires over length. This might seem a strange suggestion, but there is nothing worse that finding that when final wiring is carried out that

one wire or a pair are too short to reach their destination – believe me, I've been there!

For this project we tested all the electrics at an early stage by fitting extra long wires at each power feed position so they could be twisted together to make the whole layout live and connected to a controller without having to worry about building a control panel in the first instance. This also offers a chance to try out the layout before going too far with the project and while there is ample opportunity to make alterations and improvements.

Once we were satisfied that the electrical plan would work we proceeded with the scenic side of the project leaving the final electrical installation till last.

For all the wiring on St Stephens we have used seven strand multi-core wire. When shopping for wire two main types will be presented to you – single core and multi-core. Single core, as it sounds, as a single strand of wire inside the plastic sheathing and while perfectly acceptable for many electrical connections, it isn't best suited to model railway electrics as it becomes brittle with shaping and flexing – something which is out of the question for portable layouts and less than ideal even for home layouts.

Multi-core wire on the other hand is always a wise choice for model railway electrics. It has a series of strands inside the plastic cover which make it a better conductor as it has a greater surface area and secondly much more resilient to bending and flexing. Because there is

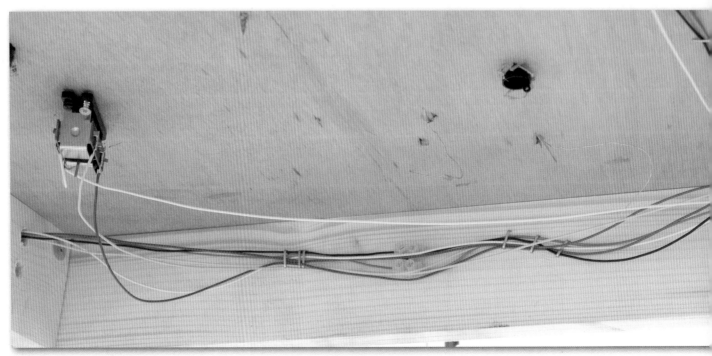

A 'Hall' 4-6-0 approaches St Stephens with a passenger working while a 'Hymek' is held at the bracket signal on the Southern route before gaining access to the Western Region line. This latter movement can be controlled by either controller plugged into the layout.

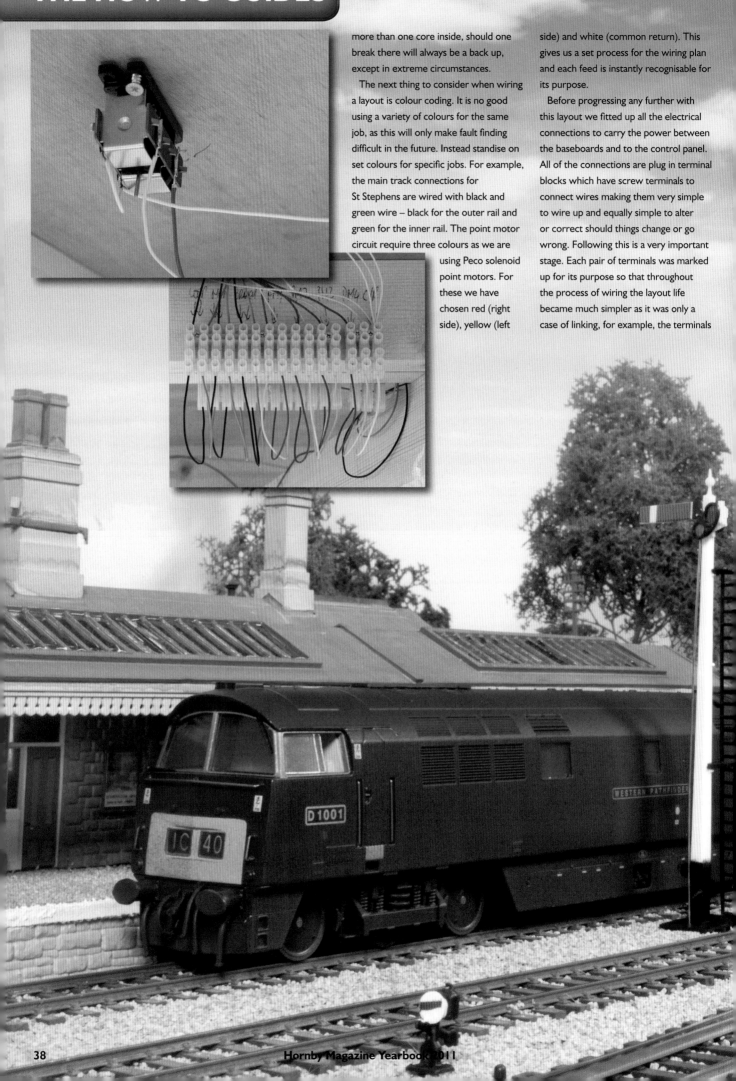

more than one core inside, should one break there will always be a back up, except in extreme circumstances.

The next thing to consider when wiring a layout is colour coding. It is no good using a variety of colours for the same job, as this will only make fault finding difficult in the future. Instead standise on set colours for specific jobs. For example, the main track connections for St Stephens are wired with black and green wire – black for the outer rail and green for the inner rail. The point motor circuit require three colours as we are using Peco solenoid point motors. For these we have chosen red (right side), yellow (left side) and white (common return). This gives us a set process for the wiring plan and each feed is instantly recognisable for its purpose.

Before progressing any further with this layout we fitted up all the electrical connections to carry the power between the baseboards and to the control panel. All of the connections are plug in terminal blocks which have screw terminals to connect wires making them very simple to wire up and equally simple to alter or correct should things change or go wrong. Following this is a very important stage. Each pair of terminals was marked up for its purpose so that throughout the process of wiring the layout life became much simpler as it was only a case of linking, for example, the terminals marked Main 1 through from its track connection point to the control panel. The process was then repeated for each connection.

The point motors were wired in a similar fashion, but for these each terminal connection was numbered with a diagram made as a reference. The numbering sequence started with PM1 – the point to the furthest left of the control panel – through to PM12 – the point furthest right of the control panel. These were then wired through to the control panel in order using the red, yellow and white colour coding previous established.

Control panel construction

The control panel for St Stephens uses 3.5mm hardboard for the top and 69mm x 18mm timber cut to length for the rear and sides. A fourth piece was cut once the panel was complete to enclose the electrical connections inside and give them further protection during transit.

On the surface of the control panel the trackplan was drawn out using a pencil and ruler with the tracks spaced at 15mm to give plenty of clearance for switches and point control studs. With this complete a second set of marks

were made for the switches and point studs before drilling holes to accept the components.

The point studs – which are Peco Lectrics components – are pushed through 2.5mm holes and have wires soldered to them underneath the panel face. These connections are then sent direct to the point motor with each stud of the each pair connecting to one side or the other of the point motor. In this case the red wire from one stud is connected to the right hand side of the point motor and the yellow wire is connected from the second stud to the left side of the motor.

To operate the points there are two more connections which are made through a Capacitor Discharge Unit (CDU). This device stores current and provides a much more positive through for point motors as it provides a short sharp burst of power.

This has a positive and negative connection – the positive connection (red) is wired to a probe (also from the Peco Lectrics range) while the negative wire (white) forms the common return which feeds directly to one side of the point motor. Don't forget to connect both terminals on one side of each point

motor together for the common return circuit. Wiring the rest of the point motors is a simple case of repeating the process of connection a red wire between a stud and the right hand side of a motor, a yellow wire between the second stud and left side of the motor and linking the white common return wire to each motor in turn.

For the switches two pairs of wire colours have been used. On the left side it is black and green and on the right it is blue and orange. These wires are linked from one switch to the next which saves on wire and also helps to tidy up the inside of the control panel. The central connections from each DPDT switch are then connected to the track as required to make the final installation.

As a final touch for St Stephens the control panel trackplan was drawn in using a black felt tip pen so that it more visible for the operators.

Keep it simple

Model railway electrics do appear, at first glance, to be complex, but my working methodically and taking your time over this part of a build it will be highly rewarding in a reliable and working railway.

Main image: A 'Western' enters the station with a through summer Saturday train.

Top left: Each of the 12 Peco point motors underneath the layout has three connections – two positive (red and yellow) and a common return feed (white) which links the two connections on the opposite side of the motor together.

Below left: Between the baseboards plug-in terminal blocks are used to make the electrical connections. These are simple to use, robust and easy to maintain.

Moving
the goods

China clay is synonymous with freight traffic in Cornwall but, as **Andrew Roden** reveals, although it was distinctive other produce was often much more important.

When it came to planning the fleet for St Stephens Road, the passenger operations were relatively straightforward, but for freight it was rather different. The sight of a '42XX' 2-8-0T or a 'Prairie' tank hauling a rake of those oh-so unusual china clay wagons with their distinctive canvas covers is inseparable from Cornwall and with Kernow Model Rail Centre's '0298' 2-4-0WT recently released, the temptation to model some china clay traffic on our layout is irresistible, but

Of course, china clay trains help identify the Cornish setting better than perhaps anything, but it is very easy to forget that although it was extremely important to the railways, the freight business wasn't dominated by it to the exclusion of everything else.

The simple fact is that up until the late 1950s and early 1960s when the branch line and station closures in the region really started to bite, railways were by far the most important form of goods transport. A huge amount of traffic travelled into Devon and Cornwall to keep the region supplied

produce such as broccoli, fruit, milk and livestock headed in the opposite direction to markets.

Neither should we forget the bulk traffic which originated in the region's tin mines (although these were largely in decline throughout the 20th century) and later at docks such as Falmouth, Plymouth and Weymouth, amongst others. For St Stephens Road to be representative, the variety of goods traffic has to reflect that of the area it served.

Inbound traffic

For incoming traffic that inevitably means that the most important load of all was coal, and transporting it was often expensive. If nothing else the GWR sourced its locomotive coal from South Wales (the cost was one of the key drivers of an aborted exploration of electrification west of Taunton in the 1930s), but with the nearest mines of any note being in Somerset, most of the coal needs of the South West were met by trains from afar. And it wasn't just needed for the railway: householders, gasworks and industry all depended on timely shipments of the black gold. It was in every sense the driving force of the South West

economy, just as it was everywhere else.

Beyond coal, there was the general merchandise needed to sustain business and communities: food, machinery for farms and factories, mechanical components, clothing and much, much more was all transported by rail in a mixture of open wagons, vans, and mail trains. The local goods workings, particularly at smaller stations of the likes of St Stephens Road, were keenly anticipated and valued, so much so that even when the branch lines lost their passenger services the freight continued to call before it was inevitably lost to road.

Although not strictly speaking freight, we shouldn't forget the trains composed entirely of empty buffet cars, which worked down to Devon and Cornwall late in the week in the summer in preparation for the mass getaways of holiday Saturdays. The pressure on siding space at these times was immense and generally speaking spare coaches were stored wherever space could be found.

Outbound traffic

The general rule for freight in Devon and Cornwall was 'coal down, produce

Left: Collett 'Grange' 4-6-0 6826 *Nannerth Grange* passes Lipsom Junction, Plymouth, with a westbound van train on September 9 1956. David Hepburne-Scott/Rail Archive Stephenson.

Below: 'Grange' 4-6-0s were regular performers on main line goods trains, but for branch lines smaller locomotives would be used such as pannier and prairie tanks and 0-6-0 designs. 'Grange' 6845 *Paviland Grange* heads an Up goods near Angarach on April 14 1960. David Hepburne-Scott/Rail Archive Stephenson.

up' and this broadly held true almost until the end of steam in early 1960s. Much of the outbound traffic was carried in the various types of general purpose open wagons and vans used on the GWR. However, some outbound cargoes, particularly agricultural, were more varied and seasonal.

Because spring arrives earlier in the South West than elsewhere, generally speaking growers had a head start on their counterparts 'up country', and the volumes carried were considerable. More than 30,000 tons of broccoli was grown in Cornwall alone every spring, equating to something in the order of 20,000 vanloads which all had to be loaded and transported in a short period of just a few weeks. Then it was on to potatoes, and then fruit and so on, not to mention the frequent livestock trains taking animals to market or slaughter as well as fish from the ports and milk, all of which had to be carried in timely and safe fashion.

Beyond agriculture there was, of course, the huge china clay traffic, sent from a myriad of freight only lines along the main lines through Devon and Cornwall, as well as to ports such as Fowey and Par. Outbound

mineral traffic such as tin ore was also significant, though declining from the end of the Great War as cheap imports made the smaller mines uneconomic.

The ever changing seasons presented a complex logistical challenge for the GWR: there was no point in sending dozens of wagons to Penzance, for example, if poor weather had extended the broccoli growing season. Doing so would clog up scarce sidings and, in any case, the odds were that the wagons could be used elsewhere. It demanded a keen eye on local conditions and flexibility to react quickly to events, as did goods from the docks and ports, which waxed and waned over the years.

Modelling the goods

From a modelling perspective, the sheer variety of traffic originating from the South West presents a mouthwatering selection of choices. Inevitably it is going to be easier to model the transition era than anything else thanks to the range of British Railways wagons which entered service. Assembling a broadly representative rake of coal, cattle or general merchandise wagons isn't going to be difficult in 'OO' scale, though in 'N' and 'O' recourse will have

On the Southern Region's North Cornwall route Maunsell 'N' 2-6-0 31842 coasts towards Camelford with an Up goods on July 26 1957. David Hepburne-Scott/Rail Archive Stephenson.

to be made to kits.

On a layout like St Stephens Road, one of the core reason for freight traffic - china clay - is straightforward in 4mm scale thanks to Bachmann's five-plank china clay wagon, which is available with and without the covers. Kernow Model Rail Centre has produced triple packs of limited edition weathered china clay wagons suitable for the 1950s and 1960s railway, while the Bachmann range features these vehicles in grey but without covers. In the BR blue diesel era these wagons were modified to feature triangular tarpaulin hoods and these were seen behind a variety of diesel locomotives.

For the BR steam era modeller adding a 'Toad' brake van (also available from Bachmann) to a short rake of clay

wagons, a 'Small Prairie' or '57XX' locomotive - perhaps double-headed given the gradients on some of the mineral railways - and you have a typical GWR/WR china clay train.

Aside from the block workings of agricultural produce and coal, many of the other freight workings were mixed, with open wagons coupled to vans, flat wagons, hoppers and more.

While many were quite long trains of 20 or more wagons, on branch lines they might be much shorter, perhaps only half a dozen wagons and a brake van. It shows that you don't necessarily need to consider lengthy goods trains by default: shorter trains are handier to operate on a model and can be completely accurate historically.

Kit manufacturers have stepped in

to offer many of the more common wagons which ran on the GWR, and with a little care in selection (book research is vital here) you can easily build up a distinctive fleet of wagons tailor made for your own model railway.

Freight power

When it comes to locomotives, it's possible to have a fair stab at creating a Cornish freight scene with off-the-shelf products, though not all are currently in production. Mixed traffic locomotives predominated in Devon and Cornwall, and although the likes of the '43XX/93XX' 2-6-0s are now fairly old models, a little detailing will bring them up to reasonable standards. Similarly, the '2251' 0-6-0s were fairly common on secondary routes, as were

While the South West is best known for its GWR motive power, the Southern Railway had a strong hold in North Cornwall where three veteran Beattie Well Tanks soldiered on specifically on china clay traffic until 1963. Beattie '0298' 2-4-0WT 30585 is about to cross the road at Boscarne with an empty clay train for Wenford Bridge on July 26 1957. David Hepburne-Scott/Rail Archive Stephenson.

the '57XX' 0-6-0PTs and '45XX/4575' 2-6-2Ts. Of the larger GWR designs, the chances of finding a 'Hall' or 'Grange' at a location such as St Stephens Road would have been remote, but a 'Manor' might conceivably have made it on a very odd occasion. In terms of diesels, the Class 22 and Class 35 diesel-hydraulics would have been the mainstays during the transition era, larger designs restricted to the main lines. It would need a little modeller's licence to justify, but Hornby's excellent '28XX' 2-8-0 would showcase the traction used on the long-haul bulk freights. But the only real absentee from the ready-to-run line-up in 'OO' scale is the '42XX' 2-8-0T, which was used on short-haul heavy freights in Cornwall. Remember too that you don't need a tender locomotive to haul a medium

length goods trains: the '57XX' 0-6-0PTs were regarded as general purpose workhorses and could haul hefty loads at good speeds.

However, while Cornwall is always remembered as being the preserve of the GWR/WR, the Southern Railway/ Region had a strong hold in North Cornwall with its routes to idylic places such as Padstow, Bude and Wadebridge. Here goods was important again with flows such as fresh fish, minerals arriving for local usage and other products arriving for consumption by the local population.

The range of motive power for Southern Region North Cornwall freights was quite diverse as these single track routes could see anything from an 'M7' 0-4-4T on light duties to a Maunsell 'N' 2-6-0 or Bulleid air-smoothed 'Light

Pacific' hauling longer trains. It should be noted that the rebuilt 'Light Pacifics' were too heavy for the North Cornwall routes.

Towards the end of Southern Region steam BR Standard designs began to appear including BR '4MT' 2-6-0 and 2-6-4Ts as well as ex-LMS Ivatt '2MT' 2-6-2Ts.

For the Great Western, as for the other three 'Big Four' railways, goods traffic was its lifeblood, and to be truly representative, the freight at St Stephens Road has to represent the community it serves, as well as the wider regional picture. To this end the two routes through our fictional station feature a wide variety of goods traffic hauled by both the Western and Southern to give the layout its reason for existence.

Left: On the Southern even 'Pacifics' would be used for goods traffic on the single track routes which weaved their way to the North Cornwall coast. On June 3 1957 'West Country' 34033 *Chard* with an Up goods near Delabole on the Padstow line. Rail Archive Stephenson.

Below: Milk traffic was an important business for the GWR and Western Region. 'Grange' 4-6-0 6800 *Arlington Grange* leaves the Royal Albert Bridge with an Up milk train in April 1951. W Verden Anderson/Rail Archive Stephenson.

Weathering
- the basics

It can be a daunting and potentially expensive prospect to pick up a can of spray paint or an airbrush to weather a model locomotive or building, but paint isn't the only way to add realism, texture and weathering stains to models. By far the most economical and easiest options to master are weathering powders in all their many and varied forms.

There are several companies producing specialist weathering powders for modellers including Carrs, through C&L Finescale, DCC Concepts and Tamiya. Carrs weathering powders are designed with the railway modeller in mind while those from Tamiya are primarily designed for military modellers. A third option is to visit a local art shop, many of which stock a range of artists pastels which can be used to weather models. Within this bracket is charcoal, another artist's medium, which is very easy to grind into a powder to add texture to a model.

There are two main types of weathering powder – oil and chalk based. Both are easy to work with, but

Continued on page 51

One of the options facing modellers looking to weather model railway rolling stock and structures is powders. **MIKE WILD** explores the world of weathering powders and compares Carrs' and Tamiya's specially designed packs with readily available artist's pastels.

STEP 1: Carrs' powders are supplied pre-ground in in packs of four colours. For this project we used the Rust and Coal, Grey Tones and Mud Tones weathering packs to re-colour the '9F'. To make the most of Carrs' weathering powders we gave this Bachmann '9F' a 'blow over' with Railmatch matt varnish from an aerosol can. Once this is done clean the wheels and test run the model again.

STEP 2: Rather than use a single colour we mixed together three hues from the Grey Tones pack plus a little coal dust from the Rust and Coal pack. The matt varnish works as a key for the powders and by working from the top down with a soft brush, a good base colour can be created. You can already see the difference between the untouched locomotive behind and the side of the tender.

STEP 3: Around the firebox we used a light grey from the Grey Tones pack to highlight the details and replicate ash stains.

STEP 4: At the front of the locomotive the same mixture of greys and coal dust colours were worked from the top down to create a base colour.

STEP 5: To add additional texture around the front footplating we wanted to add a dusting of coal dust left over from smokebox cleaning. To do this we added a few spots of matt varnish with a small paintbrush where we wanted the dust to settle.

STEP 6: Using more powder than strictly necessary the area was then covered by dipping a soft brush into the coal dust powder and tapping it over the area to cover the matt varnish.

STEP 7: The excess can then be blown away, leaving a dusting where the matt varnish was applied below.

STEP 8: Weathering steam locomotive wheels can be difficult where valve gear gets in the way. The simplest way around this is to weather what shows then return the locomotive to the rails and rotate the wheels half a turn and weather the untouched areas. These wheels have just been rotated, revealing a clean area on the first and second driving wheels. **CONTINUED...**

STEP-BY-STEP ...CONTINUED
USING CARRS'
WEATHERING POWDERS

STEP 9: To add further tones to the model, particularly rust stains, we used a combination of matt varnish and the mid colour from the Mud Tones pack to create a sludge. To do this dip a small paint brush in matt varnish and wipe off any excess on a scrap of card. Dip the varnish covered brush into a small amount of the weathering powder of your choice and then smear it onto the areas you wish to cover. Here we have highlighted some of the brake shoes and small areas of the firebox below the running plate.

STEP 10: The cylinder cover ends were treated the same way, working in a small amount of the varnish/powder mix at a time to gradually build up the effect.

STEP 11: To further enhance the overall effect a mixture of the darkest tone from the Mud Tones pack, a mid tone from the same pack and the darkest colour from the Grey Tones pack were mixed together to create a frame dirt colour. This was then applied over the tender frames and locomotive wheels to add more depth to the finished weathering job.

STEP 12: The finished '9F' suitably stained and ready for work at the head of a heavy freight.

STEP-BY-STEP USING TAMIYA WEATHERING POWDERS

STEP 1: Tamiya weathering powders are designed with military modellers in mind and they come in handy plastic packs of three colours. A small brush with a felt pad at the opposite end is also supplied in each pack to apply the powders.

STEP 2: To apply dirt to the bogie sideframes of this Class 44 we used the felt pad end of the brush wiped in the rust colour from pack 87080. This colours the frames and highlights details such as rivet heads.

STEP 3: Using the side of the felt pad makes it easy to work dirt into smaller more awkward areas.

STEP 10: Once complete you might want to set the model aside overnight and return to it the next day with fresh eyes to assess where the weathering effect can be improved. This Class 44 looks ready for the road.

STEP 4: To weather the bodyside of the Class 44 we worked in downward streaks using the felt pad. Don't be afraid to use more than one colour. The cab area of this model has rust colour streaked upwards from the bottom of the body and soot worked down from below the cab windows from pack 87080.

STEP 5: Cab fronts can be difficult to weather with the felt pad because of the amount of raised detail. To make the most of the Tamiya powders in areas like this it is best to use the brush to work the powders into panel lines and around other small details.

STEP 6: Cab roofs tend to weather quickly in service and the Tamiya powders can recreate the streaked effect of accumulated dirt, rain water and general grime well when added from the cab windows backwards.

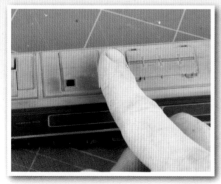

STEP 7: As well as using the supplied pad, fingers are very useful for smearing and spreading powders across bodysides and roofs.

STEP 8: Remember that exhaust ports will have more dirt around them. To replicate this we added a second colour over the main soot colour in the form of oil staining from pack 87088. This was applied with the felt pad and then smoothed with finger pressure.

STEP 9: By using the side of the felt pad, oil streaks can be added to the sides of models. This oil stain has been added using pack 87088.

THE HOW TO GUIDES

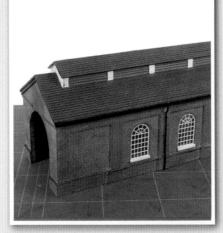

STEP 1: For this guide we have used a Bachmann Scenecraft locomotive shed as the base model. An optional first step is to matt varnish the building which will add a further key for the weathering powders on application. However, if you choose to do this the windows will need to be covered with masking tape as matt varnish adds a frosting to glazing.

STEP 2: To weather this building we mixed two colours from Carrs' powders together – coal dust and the darkest shade from the Grey Tones pack. These were then mixed together with a brush before application.

STEP 3: A prominent area for weathering on a building like this is above the entrance where locomotive exhausts will stain the brickwork. This area was already lightly weathered from the factory, but in our view benefitted from extra staining.

STEP 4: Working along the side of the building the powders were worked from the corners of each section making sure ledges gained a suitable coating.

STEP 5: The roof of this building weathered very nicely with powders. Working in downward strokes the effect can be built up with several thin layers to the coal dust and dark grey powder mixture.

STEP 6: To make the building appear a little more run down and used moss stains were added to the roof using the darkest green from Carrs' Spring Greens weathering powders pack.

the oil based versions can be smeared more easily while the chalk based versions are more suited to adding dusty effects.

The weathering powders produced by Carrs' and Tamiya are both oil based and can be used in a number of ways including brushing onto models and smearing with felt pads or finger tips. Carrs' weathering powders can also be streaked during application or worked as a sludge with matt varnish (see panel).

From working with the two companies' products we found that Carrs' offered the most potential in terms of the variety of colours available, the way they adhere to models and also their versatility. Artists pastels, in our view, also offer a similar level of potential, but require a little more forethought to make the most of them.

As a general rule most weathering powders will adhere better to a matt paint finish than gloss. Gloss finishes tend to be too slippery for weathering powders and the simplest way around this is to blow a light coat of matt varnish onto a model from an aerosol before starting work with powders. If you are building kits then it is also possible to paint the model with matt paints and we have also found that acrylics, which tend to have a semi matt finish, provide a good base for powder weathering.

With this in mind it is a good idea to start by practicing techniques on cheap models rather than starting out with a brand new ready-to-run locomotive. We recommend purchasing a small selection of second hand wagons or cheap road vehicles as a starting point to practice the application of matt varnish (if you haven't used it before) and also the weathering powders.

It is also worth remembering to cover or remove windows from models when spraying with matt varnish as it will add an unwanted frosting to glazing which can affect the finished result.

The steps in the panels will show you how we go about weathering locomotives, rolling stock and building with weathering powders as well as illustarting the methods we use for the different types of powder.

If you are unsure about weathering powders the best thing we can say is have a go. Take the plunge with an inexpensive item of stock, try different techniques, adapt what we show here. It's all about trialling ideas and that is what makes weathering so enjoyable.

Improving a GWR railcar

The GWR railcar is a complete train in one coach and is highly useful to the compact layout builder. **Phil Parker** takes a Hornby BR liveried railcar and adds a few personal touches to make it stand out from the crowd.

Railcars are the answer to the space starved modeller's prayer - an entire, scale length passenger train in around a foot yet suitable for nearly every type of layout. Most companies experimented with both steam and diesel versions for lightly trafficked branch lines but it's probably the GWR which produced the most iconic designs. Built in two batches, the first were produced by the Gloucester Railway Carriage and Wagon Company whilst later versions, to a more angular design, came from Swindon works in 1940. All survived into BR ownership and three vehicles have been preserved. The story of the GWR railcars feature on pages 106-109 of this book.

When Lima introduced its ready-to-run model in the very early 1980s it was very well received with the unusual looks nicely modelled. It's been a staple on many layouts since then and now appears in the Hornby range. As with the other reintroductions from Lima, an upgrade of the mechanical side has taken place with a smooth running bogie replacing the pancake motor. The old Lima power unit tended to be either good or bad and if you got a bad one there wasn't much you could do about it until ModelTorque produced upgrades a few years ago. The wheels weren't much to shout about either, normally being derisively termed 'pizza cutters' thanks to the deep flanges. Of course these can be replaced as well if you have the older model and there are plenty of these about on the second hand market.

My plan for this project had been simple: wire handrails, replacement roof vents

The story of the GWR railcars feature on pages 106-109 of this book.

STEP-BY-STEP UPGRADING A HORNBY GWR RAILCAR

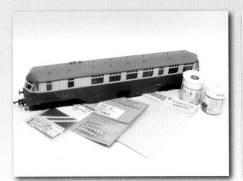

STEP 1: Railcar and detailing parts – the parts used in this project are a flush glaze kit, whitemetal vents and steam pipes along with touch up paints. To this collection I added some seated people and brass wire.

STEP 2: Disassembly starts by carefully pulling the buffers out of the ends. These need quite a tug so don't pull the heads or they might come off. Then undo the two crosshead screws near the bogies. Finally, unclip the body from the chassis by flexing the sides.

STEP 3: File a little flat on the top of each vent, then drill it through the centre. This makes it easy to keep each hole in the middle of the vent. Finally, carve and sand away the remains of the moulded vent.

SUPPLIERS

- Gibson 0.31mm straight brass wire - **£2.50** for 10 lengths (Eileens Emporium)
- Scalloped dome vents - **£2.20** (Dart Castings)
- Seated people - **£6.30** (Slaters)
- Screw coupling - **£4.08** (Kenrow Model Rail Centre)
- Steam/Vacuum pipes - **£2.00** (Shawplan)
- Hornby Carmine paint RC423 - **£1.44**
- Hornby Cream paint RC424 - **£1.44**

Total: £19.96

The finished BR carmine and cream railcar now features detailed bufferbeams, a weathered finish plus passengers and a driver.

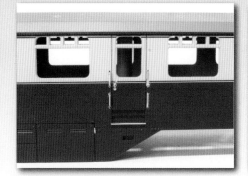

STEP 4: With a sharp blade, remove the ends of the handrails. Use this as a guide to show where the holes for the replacement wire versions should go. Then remove the rest of the moulding. Work carefully to avoid having touch up too much of the paintwork.

STEP 5: At the front, the area with the moulded coupling isn't deep enough but is easily removed. While I was at it, the little handrails under the windscreen disappeared and the mould lines around the lights.

STEP 6: The Hornby acrylic paints are a really excellent match for the colours used on the model. The black buffer beam took a couple of coats but the damage left by handrail removal was gone with a single flick of a brush.

The finished railcar ready to take to the rails on St Stephens Road.

and some flush glazing.

Examining prototype photographs, the handrails appear to be finer than on most rolling stock. This might be an optical illusion but to be on the safe side I opted for 0.31mm straight brass wire rather than the 0.45mm I'd normally use for an 'OO' model.

Roof vents are interesting and poorly represented on the model. Both torpedo and clam vents appear to have been fitted to the prototype. I opted for the later as they could be clearly seen in a couple of photographs but whichever you prefer, the method for fitting is the same.

Flush glazing gave me the biggest problem. I don't know if the body

moulding has changed slightly since Lima days, maybe the paint used now is thicker than in the past, but I couldn't make the normally excellent Wills Flushglaze fit. The main windows were fine but none of the toplights would go in. It wasn't for want of trying either, I ruined several glazing units trying to force them into too small a hole.

To add to this, around the front, the angled windscreens are particularly difficult for the vacuum-forming process that produces the glazing. To use the glazing in the cab you'll need to largely remove the sides and figure out something for the sliding side windows which have been represented with paint on the Hornby glazing unit – Lima simply ignored them!

After many attempts, including experimenting with Krystal-Klear to replace the small panes, I chickened out and went back to the supplied plastic glazing. It's not as good as good flush glazing but better than a half-hearted attempt would have been. I've always worked on the basis that any detailing

has to improve on the supplied item and I don't think this would have been the case here. It's a pity as flush-glazing would really lift this model. Perhaps there is an opening for another manufacturer to produce a new kit to suit the Hornby GWR railcar?

One thing I was pleasantly surprised at was the quality of the Hornby acrylic paint used to touch up the body sides after the removal of handrails. The colour match is excellent – not always something you can take for granted. The actual shades are the subject of a bit of debate since contemporary photographs aren't that reliable but at least Hornby has picked a colour and stuck to it.

Because of this, the project is particularly suitable for beginners since it's easy to hide any damage when removing moulded items. In fact there really isn't much to worry about at all yet once you've managed these tweaks you'll gain in confidence and start eyeing up all sorts of rolling stock for a quick upgrade.

USEFUL LINKS - *SUPPLIER WEBSITES*

STEP 7: Replacing the vents is simply a case of gluing the new white metal items in place. Do check that they are all the same way around before the glue dries, these aren't simple domes but domed covers with vents in the sides and the vents facing along the roof.

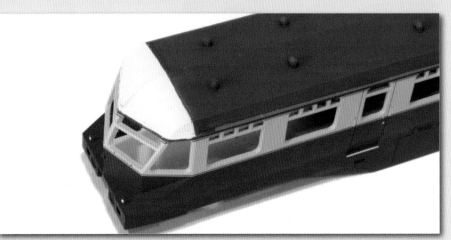

STEP 8: The roof looked too light in colour to me compared to photographs so I gave it a coat of Humbrol 66. While I was at it, most of the photographs showed the domed fronts to be white so I masked this and painted it in the correct colour.

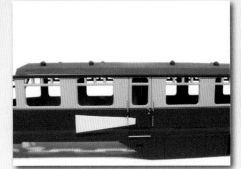

STEP 9: Handrails are made from 0.31mm diameter wire bent and fitted in the holes. A sliver of scrap plasticard about three quarters of a millimetre thick is used as a spacer to make sure the distance the rails were away from the sides was consistent. You can do it by eye, but with a spacer this is a lot simpler.

STEP 10: As mentioned in the main text, the Flushglaze pack didn't seem to fit properly. The main windows were fine but the little ones didn't work at all. I tried only using the big pane and used Krystal Klear in the top but while it looks acceptable in this photograph, the reality wasn't nearly as nice since the top pane isn't as flush as the bottom one.

STEP 11: Inside the seats were painted a red rust colour, sides wood and floor a dusty earth. Glazing the partition windows was an experiment that I wouldn't bother repeating as you can't tell once the model is reassembled.

STEP 12: Slaters plastic people require their lower legs to be removed to fit in the seats. If you are operating with DCC, now's the time to remove the blanking plug and put the chip in.

STEP 13: The Jackson screw couplings are a bit chunky as they are working items, but they fit easily enough if you drill a hole for the shank. In the same way the white metal pipe goes on the left with the other pipe made from a bit of paperclip since it has a smooth cover.

STEP 14: Reassembled, the finished model just needs a bit of weathering around the bogies to be ready for service. Start with a coat of Railmatch weathered black and follow up with some weathering powders.

Building
a Ratio station
building

What's the first building that people look at on a model railway? The chances are it's the station. **Phil Parker** tackles the Ratio GWR station building kit to create the focal point for St Stephens Road. *Photography, Phil Parker.*

WHAT WE USED

Component	Supplier	Cat No.	Price
GWR station building	Ratio	504	£26.30
GWR platform canopy	Ratio	515	£13.10

● *Ratio building kits are available from model shops nationwide.*

Unless you have something really spectacular on your layout, its focal point will most likely be the station building. This makes sense as this is the place where in real life most of us interact with the railway. Even if the model isn't a prototype we are familiar with in real life, we all know the features and have a rough idea of how the building should be laid out.

Station buildings come in a huge variety of shapes and sizes. In the UK we have never gone for identical buildings, (I don't count the modern bus-shelter as a building) although architectural styles are sometimes reasonably consistent along a line, especially if it was built in pre-grouping days when the builders wanted to make their mark.

For this reason, there aren't that many kits available, but one of the oldest is from Ratio. It has been available in some form for at least 25 years judging by the cover of the 1983 catalogue. The box title might be simply Station Building, but in fact it's a pretty accurate model of Castle Cary station on the Reading to Taunton line in Somerset. Every year the real site becomes the focus for travellers

to the Glastonbury festival, which would present an interesting challenge.

With this model being destined for St Stephens Road, I didn't have to worry too much about it being an accurate model of a particular structure as the layout is freelance, but I still wanted to personalise it if possible to be in keeping with the area of the layout's location. The easiest way to do this was by painting the stonework in the appropriate hue. An hour spent looking at stone buildings in the locale on the web showed that this could be anything from iron red through sandstone beige to a slate blue where the weather had really got at it. In the end,

a creamy beige was chosen as much for attractiveness as prototype fidelity.

Despite being a small model, there are lots of parts and it's very sensible to paint the model as it's constructed. I assembled all the walls and painted them with a pale grey (Humbrol 64) and then dry-brushed Humbrol 83 (Ochre) over the stone tops. Doing this quickly, before the first colour has fully dried, allows the paint to blend a little softening both colours. Ochre might seem a bit dark but my next move was to work talcum powder over the model with a stiff brush. This lightens the colour further and as an added bonus some powder sticks to

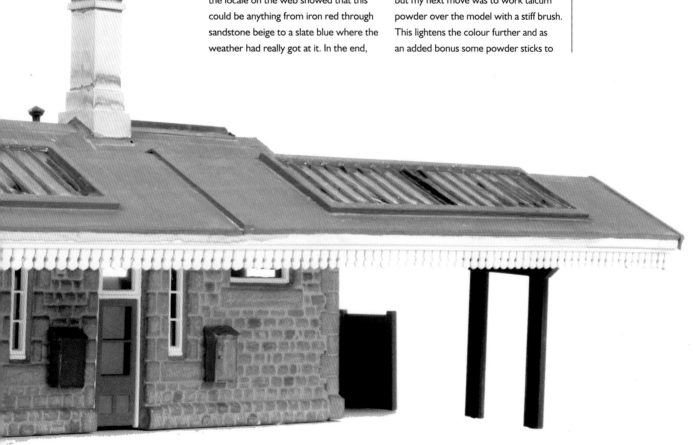

The brickwork is heavily detailed with painting techniques as described in the step by step guide.

STEP-BY-STEP — BUILDING THE RATIO GWR STATION BUILDING

STEP 1: The modest sized box is full of different coloured sprues. Be careful not to lose some of the smaller separate components.

STEP 2: The walls are made up of several parts. Corners are braced using fillet mouldings. If you plan to detail the interior, leave these out as they will be in the way. Careful handling of the part built model means they aren't essential and once the roof is glued on, the structure will be nice and strong.

STEP 3: Before assembling any corner, the quoins (cornerstones) are fitted, then the walls can be brought together. Do it the other way around and the quoins don't fit! Check everything is flat and square at this point - any problems and fitting the roof will be difficult.

STEP 4: The channel running around the edges of the quoins is grouted with PVA glue applied with a small brush. The thicker the glue the better – Resin W worked well for me.

STEP 5: To give the stonework a bit of texture I rubbed talcum powder into the surface once the paint was touch dry. This ensures a matt finish.

STEP 6: The roof is in two sections with the join in the middle of a panel. A little filling and smoothing with fine sandpaper was required to make this invisible. Once fitted the supporting beam for the canopy is added with side tagged A against the wall, remove the tag first though.

STEP 7: The chimneys are made up of a surprising number of parts. At the bottom edges I found a little filler was necessary. For more variety, the pots could be replaced with whitemetal aftermarket components.

STEP 8: To blend the chimneys and skylight into the roof I cut some thin strips of paper to represent the lead flashing. Stick this in place with several washes of liquid plastic glue. As well as being prototypical, the 'flashing' hides any little gaps.

STEP 9: Canopy construction starts by fitting the roof panels together, they are identical in size so you can have the skylights in any configuration you want. When dry, fit the ends and then the intermediate girders.

STEP 10: On each side of every girder are four plates. Two types are supplied and the instructions show which one to fit to the correct sides. Next, the girders are fitted. Keep looking along the model to ensure these are in a straight line.

give the plastic stonework offering a little texture. Finally some of the stones were picked out with a slightly reddish colour and talc'd again. The result looks pleasant enough, just the thing for a picturesque place like St Stephens.

Pre-painting continued with all the doors, windows and guttering. It's just easier to work while parts are still attached to the sprue than glue them in place only to have to try and work around them on the model. Mind you, it took many years for me to realise this!

One piece of advice I will give for this kit – read the instructions. They are detailed and if you follow them carefully, a quality model will be the result. This isn't the simplest kit in the world and if you don't pay attention, you can trip over yourself. I know - I did. For example, I assumed that the corners of the wall would be stuck together and then the decorative stonework (quoins) glued over this. Do that and the quoins don't fit, they have to go on first, as it says in the instructions.

While on the subject of the corners, they don't initially appear to fit very well with a groove around the edges. As the manufacturers suggests, pointing this with PVA works ever so well, completely filling the gaps and bedding the two components together. It's a technique I'll use again.

Finally, as this model was destined to be delivered to the *Hornby Magazine* office, a 90 mile drive away from where I built it, I didn't attach the canopy or gents toilet screen properly as they would probably get knocked off in transit and possibly damaged. Final assembly of these parts is better handled once the building is on the layout. It will certainly make bedding the base into the platform a lot easier.

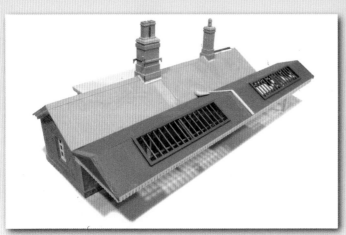

STEP 11: On the front of the building support mainly comes from the girder fitted at Step 6. For the far end a leg is supplied which appears to fit in the middle of a girder. Photographs of the real building appear to show it fitted at the back. It's your choice as either will work well. Until the canopy is glued to the building it isn't self-supporting, hence the Blu-tack in this test.

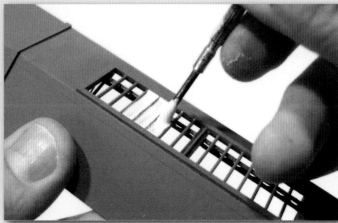

STEP 12: With the girders fitted you can't easily slide plastic in to glaze the skylights so I used Microscale Kristal Klear. It's a high quality PVA that dries clear. Just fill the aperture with it from the end of a screwdriver. Keep the pane flat while the liquid dries.

STEP 13: Poster boards were filled with real railway advertising found on the web and printed out at a suitable size. Alternatively, several suppliers can provide something suitable. Bright and bold designs work best in model form.

STEP 14: All the windows have been glazed with plastic sheet stuck in place with PVA. Superglue and plastic cement tend to fog the glazing unless used very sparingly.

STEP 15: At one end of the building is the screen around the gents toilet door. This will be fixed when the building is fitted to the platform, it's far to weak a joint otherwise.

STEP 17: The canopy is available as a standalone kit for extending that on the station or for other platforms. The kit is the same apart from the inclusion of some legs to support it.

STEP 16: In this form it's ideal for an island platform. If you want to use it to extend the station canopy, remove the detail from one end to get them to butt together properly.

Gallery

A Gresley 'A4' class 'Pacific' races through Gamston with an express and overtakes a 'WD' 2-8-0 on the goods loop while another freight heads in the opposite direction. John Houlden's Gamston Bank featured in HM46. Trevor Jones.

A Bulleid 'Q1' threads along the embankment at Rowland's Castle while below the American military prepare for the onset of invasion. This is Southern England in 1944. Peter Goss' Rowland's Castle featured in HM44. Mike Wild

A Maunsell 'N' 2-6-0 restarts its mixed goods from Ashland – the layout built in a weekend by the *Hornby Magazine* team at Hornby Magazine LIVE! in Hartlepool in 2011. Ashland featured in HM51. Mike Wild.

Hamwick Lane basks in the evening light of the moon in a scene which combines Bob Petch's superb modelling and a real sky. Shillinghurst and Hamwick Lane featured in HM52.

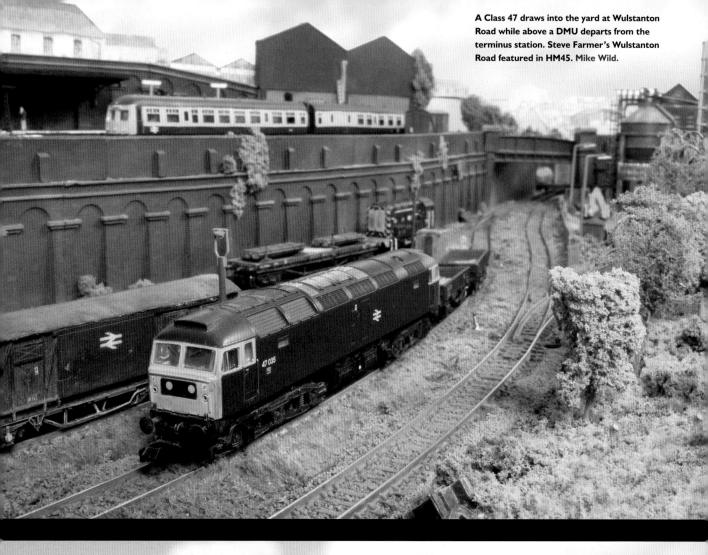

A Class 47 draws into the yard at Wulstanton Road while above a DMU departs from the terminus station. Steve Farmer's Wulstanton Road featured in HM45. Mike Wild.

The time is the mid-1950s and the place is the Settle and Carlisle. The English Electric prototype *Deltic* thunders through Hettle and passes a 'Jubilee' at the head of a Northbound express. Hettle featured in HM48 and *Hornby Magazine Yearbook No. 3*. Mike Wild.

A 'WD' 2-8-0 passes a classmate on the curved viaduct at Tetley Mills while hauling a long rake of empty coal wagons. Dave Shakespeare's Tetley Mills featured in HM50. Mike Wild.

In the desolate hills of the
Pennine hills two BR '9F' 2-10-0s
cross paths at Irebridge Junction
with steel and coal workings.
Halifax Model Railway Club's
Irebridge Junction featured in
HM42. Mike Wild.

Branching out

The Great Western branch line terminus has become a modelling cliché, but as **Andrew Roden** reveals, the variety of appearance and operation was immense, creating some captivating possibilities for railway modellers.

I t is said that more words have been written about the Great Western Railway than any other railway in history, and countless authors, myself included, have tried with varying degrees of success to analyse the company's extraordinary appeal. However, if you ask the average club railway modeller about the appeal of building a GWR branch line terminus you are guaranteed to provoke a strong response.

For many years after the Second World War, the most popular type of model railway by far was a small branch line terminus set somewhere in the West Country or South West, a fair way away from the village it purported to serve but with a bewildering variety of traffic nonetheless. So popular were these layouts that even the description 'Great Western branch line terminus' has become something of a cliché.

I suppose that a terminus like Ashburton, Devon, is the kind of image many modellers have in mind when they envisage a GWR branch line. A small single platform station with enclosing timber train shed serving a small town; a single road engine shed, some goods facilities and glorious summer sunshine complete an enticing picture. Of course, the Great Western (like the Southern Railway too) did have a lot of termini thanks to its routes in Dorset, Devon and Cornwall but inevitably these were vastly outnumbered by the cross-country waypoints on secondary routes which criss-crossed the country like a fabric weave.

Some of the GWR's lesser routes have passed into legend: the Didcot, Newbury & Southampton, Severn Valley, Oxford, Worcester and Wolverhampton, as well as branches such as the seven-mile line from Tiverton Junction to Hemyock, and the web of routes in the Forest of Dean are all well known and documented. The paradox is that far from being virtually identical as modelling lore would have it, the only thing these railways have in common is that they are very different from each other!

Building identity

The reason for the differences are primarily historical. Purists will rightly point out that the Great Western Railway itself built very few branch lines: those between London and Reading and odd fill-in routes aside, the vast majority of

Above: Ex-GWR '14XX' 0-4-2T 1451 pauses at Hemyock with the 1.42pm from Tiverton Junction on August 8 1962. Mike Fox/Rail Archive Stephenson.

Left: Not all branch line trains on the Western Region network were handled by ex-GWR locomotives. Ex-LMS Ivatt '2MT' 2-6-2T 41208 calls at Wells Priory Road with the 2pm from Yatton on June 16 1962. Mike Fox/Rail Archive Stephenson.

the company's secondary routes were acquired by takeover or amalgamation. The differences can be profound as two examples show. Buckfastleigh station was built by the Buckfastleigh, Totnes and South Devon Railway in 1872, only becoming part of the GWR in 1897. Codsall station, in Shropshire, meanwhile, was built by the Shrewsbury and Birmingham Railway in 1849, and although it merged with the GWR five years later, its buildings were very different. Both stations spent the majority of their pre-nationalisation existences owned by the GWR, but neither were of GWR origin.

It may seem a small point, but the differences in appearance between stations across the GWR network were profound. The signage was similar, as was the tightly controlled corporate identity (which is why at a superficial glance the company's routes do look similar). Nonetheless, only the small unmanned halts with their distinctive pagoda shelters could be found across the company's network. In so far as it is possible to say so, there was no such thing as a typical GWR country station.

Operations

One of the reasons that the GWR was so popular amongst railway modellers of the 1940s and 1950s was the external simplicity of its locomotives. With clean lines and simple outside motion it was much easier to build an acceptable model from scratch than a more complex design from another of the 'Big Four' companies. That the GWR made such extensive use of short trains of one or two coaches behind a tank locomotive was another welcome bonus for modellers of the time.

Again though, the assertion that all GWR secondary routes looked the same in terms of operations is wide of the mark. Certainly the locomotives were green, and post 1923 and up to nationalisation in 1948 most if not all of the carriages were painted chocolate and cream, but the variety of locomotive classes and carriages in use was bewildering and a real minefield for modellers seeking total authenticity.

One might imagine that the versatile '57XX' 0-6-0PTs predominated on

branch lines but there were many where their fixed wheelbase was simply too long such as the Gwinear Road to Helston branch. Similarly, other routes were very steeply graded, so on lines like Yelverton to Princetown or Wellington to Craven Arms the '44XX' 2-6-2Ts (which were built with 4ft 1½in diameter driving wheels) held sway. Elsewhere, the similar '45XX' 2-6-2Ts, which had slightly larger 4ft 7½in driving wheels, were common - and of course, the delightful '48XX' (later '14XX') 0-4-2Ts and their '517' class predecessors were regular sights too.

As one would expect given the preponderance of tank locomotives in the GWR fleet, tank engines predominated on large swathes of GWR secondary routes but tender locomotives were important on many of them too. The versatile '43XX' and '93XX' 2-6-0s were often seen on goods and passenger trains from the South West to Mid Wales, while the 'Manor' 4-6-0s were designed specifically for lightly laid routes which demanded relatively high power and

Left: GWR diesel railcar W16W stands at Faringdon on a special working for the Southall Railway Club on April 24 1955. J Davies/Rail Archive Stephenson.

Main: With the terrace houses of the Welsh Valleys behind, '57XX' 0-6-0PT 3767 leaves Bedwas with a Brecon to Newport working on May 9 1959. Bob Tuck/Rail Archive Stephenson.

endurance. We shouldn't forget the 'Dukedog' 4-4-0s of the late 1930s either when considering mid-Wales, not to mention the Dean and Collett 0-6-0s.

Strange finds

Even in the 1950s there were some distinct oddities roaming the former GWR network, such as the 11 ex-Cambrian Railways '15' class 0-6-0s, a plethora of tank locomotives from the South Wales railways which were amalgamated with the GWR in 1923, and the three former Midland & South Western Junction Railway 2-4-0s which seldom strayed far from the Lambourn branch.

The picture gets more complicated the further back in time. Venture back to the late 1920s and with the Churchward/Collett standardisation programme still far from completion, it becomes possible to model many of the 4-4-0 designs of around the turn of the century which eked out their final years on secondary duties. There were many variations on the 0-6-0 theme in both tank and tender locomotive form, as well as 'Stella' and 'Barnum' 2-4-0s and a panoply of rare and unusual locomotives from constituent companies. The GWR of the 1920s must have been a dazzling and at times disorienting spectacle to those of us used to more homogenised fleets.

If anything, carriages and wagons are even more complicated, with four-wheel non-corridor clerestory vehicles in service into the 1930s as well as the advanced designs of Churchward and Collett. Of course,

autocoaches provide a solid base for many passenger services but for other locomotive hauled trains, cascaded older stock would have been used, rendering a truly accurate portrayal of the GWR extremely difficult. Thankfully, by the mid-1950s to mid-1960s period which seems to be most popular at the moment amongst modellers, the coaching side of things had settled down, with secondary services largely formed of coaches of Churchward and Collett designs. Of course, the railcars introduced from the 1930s add a different complexion too, and while there were never enough of them to be ubiquitous, they did appear, as Evan Green-Hughes demonstrates on pages 106-109, frequently on lesser lines.

Freight traffic obviously varied by season and region, but as with all railways, coal was the most predictable commodity, with most stations receiving at least a couple of wagons on a regular basis. Model railways set in South Wales would need to have coal as the main traffic, far ahead of passenger and other freight services. Agriculture provided varying traffic flows throughout the year, with flowers from the Isles of Scilly followed by fruit and vegetables as their growing seasons started. Some of these flows were connected with specific areas: Cornish broccoli, plums from Worcestershire, lamb from Wales and so on, while others such as grain were more wide ranging but still important.

We shouldn't forget the general pick-up goods trains which until the end of the 1950s carried the produce and materials needed to sustain

Top left: While tank engines dominated many GWR branch lines, larger locomotives were required in some areas. On August 30 1961 '43XX' 2-6-0 7333 leaves the 246 yard Venn Cross tunnel and approaches Venn Cross station with freight for Barnstaple. Mike Fox/Rail Archive Stephenson.

Below left: GWR 'Dukedog' 4-4-0 9003 calls at Penryndeudraeth with a Barmouth to Pwlheli train formed of ex-LMS and ex-GWR stock in the early 1950s. Gordon Hepburn/Rail Archive Stephenson.

Below: '57XX' 0-6-0PT 5779 leaves Minehead – now the terminus of the preserved West Somerset Railway - with a pick-up goods for Taunton on August 29 1961. Mike Fox/Rail Archive Stephenson.

The driver of GWR '14XX' 1469 watches from the cab at Churston as a sister engine propels a motor train from Brixham into the station on June 26 1952. Stan Garth/Rail Archive Stephenson.

communities - from the smallest consignment to the biggest load which could fit under the railway's bridges and tunnels, the railways carried the lot, and the GWR was no exception.

Modelling the GWR

The immense variety in appearance and operations of GWR secondary routes and branches means that there is huge scope for building interesting and entertaining model railways as far removed from the clichés of railway modelling past as it is possible to imagine.

In practical terms there are big arguments against choosing a terminus as a subject, not least because they took up a huge amount of space, as pictures of the likes of Princetown - a horribly remote station show. This was because land in rural areas was relatively cheap so there was little incentive to compress operations. By contrast, urban stations are generally much more compact. A further consideration is that even a small through station can be more interesting to operate than a terminus.

Modelling the GWR or British Railways

Western Region is not without its pitfalls. Using a stock GWR building kit for a station, for example, is chancy unless you know it depicts stations from the area you intend to model. A little research - and thankfully, sources on the GWR are legion - can make the difference between a general pastiche of the GWR which never truly satisfies and something much more embedded in reality, whether the model is of a prototype or not.

Similarly, introducing variety to the rolling stock requires a little research but can pay huge dividends by allowing a much wider fleet than you might expect. The major classes of locomotive are covered by the mainstream manufacturers in 'OO' scale, but GWR coaching stock is a little thin on the ground at the moment. Even so, if you're prepared to dip your toes into the realm of kit building, there are enough

tantalising prototypes to justify some really different locomotives on your layout. With a little modeller's licence, you could even justify the likes of a 'King' 4-6-0 if your layout is set in the right area: some were sent over the Tamar to stable in Cornwall during the Second World War to prevent them being bombed, so there is a precedent.

As we've seen, there wasn't really such a thing as a typical Great Western branch line, but that lingering echo of the company's secondary routes continue to exert a massive pull on the consciousnesses of railway modellers all over the world.

Review ● of the Year 2010-2011

The past 12 months have seen an explosion of stunning locomotives from ready-to-run manufacturers. **Mike Wild** looks back at the new releases between September 2010 and August 2011 in this Review of the Year.

Above: Bachmann's Fowler '7F' 2-8-0 arrived December 2010.

Below: Hornby's Thompson 'L1' 2-6-4T arrived in September 2010.

Right: Bachmann debuted its Class 03 diesel shunter in 2010.

Locomotives and rolling stock are what makes this hobby tick and the past 12 months has seen an impressive range of new models arrive for 'N', 'OO' and 'O' gauge ranging from humble goods wagons to the most impressive locomotives. However, it hasn't just been about producing new models – our manufacturers and retailers have been announcing more products to whet our appetites.

The past two years have been exceptionally exciting for railway modellers. The rise and rise of the commission market where retailers are having exclusive models produced as accelerated the growth of the range, and particularly for 'OO' gauge.

'OO' is by far and away still the market leader in terms of product development, but 'N' gauge isn't far behind at the moment. In some ways 'N' gauge is making greater strides as Bachmann and Dapol develop new mechanisms, improve detail and grow their ranges.

Turn the clock back just five years and it was a very different picture. Then product development was the preserve of the major manufacturers and while the availability and variety of models grew, it was nothing like the pace that has become almost normality in the past two years. Add into this a selection of reliveries on existing models and each year becomes more and more tantalising and exciting.

September 2010

The first new model to be announced in this period was an all-new 'N' gauge Thompson 'B1' 4-6-0 from Bachmann. This followed on from Dapol's announcement of the same locomotive and at the time both were due to arrive in the country within weeks of each other.

Alongside this new item *Hornby Magazine* revealed the first pre-production images of the LMS Stove R van, Kernow showed the first shots of its Beattie '0298' 2-4-0WT, while Realtrack Models showed the latest CAD/CAM

artwork for its Class 144. Similarly Olivia's Trains revealed CAD/CAM images of it Class 76 EM1 electric and Dapol showed the first shots of its Class 43 HST power cars and liveried samples of its newly announced 'B1' 4-6-0.

That though was just the tip of the iceberg as September also saw Hornby release the first of its promised Thompson 'L1' 2-6-4Ts together with its new range of ex-GWR Hawksworth coaches and a new version of the 'King Arthur' with a Drummond water cart

tender. Meanwhile Bachmann raised the bar for shunting locomotives with its brand new Class 03 diesel shunter and 'N' gauge benefitted from the first of Bachmann's new Mk 1 coaches.

October 2010

Leading the news in October was Heljan. During the month it revealed production samples of BRCW prototype D0260 *Lion* together with pre-production models of its Class 23 'Baby Deltic' for 'OO' and it 'O' gauge production 'Deltic'. Kernow

also showed the popularity of its Beattie Well Tank by announcing that it had almost sold out almost a year before its arrival.

New releases were a feast for Eastern Region modellers. In 'OO' Bachmann launched its Peppercorn 'A2' 4-6-2 while Dapol's new 'N' gauge 'B1' 4-6-0 also touched down. Golden Age Models sublime Gresley 'A4' 4-6-2s also arrived in the *Hornby Magazine* office while in 'N' gauge Bachmann released its new Class 14 diesel hydraulic.

Also arriving during October was Hornby's Railroad Class 40 which used the ex-Lima body tooling with an upgraded DCC ready chassis and a power-twin Class 108 DMU for 'N' gauge from Bachmann.

November 2010

The Warley National Model Railway Exhibition became a hot bed for new announcements with Dapol revealing plans for English Electric prototype DP2 and a Class 21/29 North British Type 2 for 'OO' gauge while Heljan announced a Class 128 Gloucester parcels railcar for 'OO' and a Brush Class 31 for 'O' gauge. Warley also provided the first chance to see progress on Heljan's Waggon und Machinenbau railbus, the Hattons/Heljan Class 28, Heljan's 'O' gauge Class 26, 33 and 55, Bachmann's 'N' gauge Class 101 and Class 03 plus Dapol's 'OO' gauge

Class 22 and Model Rail's Sentinel. Also shown were pre-production samples of Bachmann's 2-EPB EMU, Fowler '7F' 2-8-0 and Class 70 diesel together with an early mock-up of Bachmann's model of LMS prototype diesels 10000/10001. Hornby took the opportunity to showcase development of its 4-VEP third-rail EMU together with its OTA timber wagons and KFA container flats while Dapol debuted pre-production samples of its Class 121 and Class 142 DMUs for 'N' gauge. Another highlight was the first look at the CAD/CAM artwork for the Hatton's/Dapol models of LMS 10000/10001.

New releases were crowned by Bachmann's latest 'N' gauge offerings covering the Thompson 'B1' 4-6-0 and English Electric prototype *Deltic* plus the new 'N' gauge Travelling Post Office van arrived for the scale too.

In 'OO' Bachmann released its IPA car carrier and Hornby's 'County' 4-6-0 returned in the Railroad range.

December 2010

The final month of the year is always one of excitement with Hornby announcing its plans for the following year at Christmas. A strong range of new items were revealed by Hornby with a new Railroad model of new build 'Pacific' 60163 *Tornado* leading a line up which also featured a new Thompson 'B1' 4-6-0, the 'Brighton Belle' 5-BEL EMU, a GWR horsebox, a BR 20ton brake van, BR 27ton tippler, a North Eastern Railway Trout ballast hopper, Gresley suburban stock and a Gresley full brake in terms of rolling stock.

In other areas Hornby announced its would be launching new software called RailMaster to allow computer

control of a model railway through the manufacturer's Elite DCC controller and TrackMaster – a new layout planning programme.

December was also exceptionally busy for new releases. In 'OO' gauge Bachmann lead the way with its Fowler '7F' 2-8-0, Eastern Region box vans and 13ton steel sided open wagons while Hornby was hot on its heels with the GWR '2884' 2-8-0 arriving together with the DCC sound fitted 'Schools' 4-4-0. The National Railway Museum also revealed its limited edition Great Central Railway liveried 'O4' 2-8-0 and Bachmann released its Autoballaster wagon too.

In 'O' gauge Heljan's new Class 33 arrived offering Southern Region modellers something new for the larger scale. Only the Class 33/0 has been produced in 'O' by Heljan.

January 2011

The year started with Hatton's revealing the first pre-production sample of 10000 together with the first liveried sample of its Heljan produced Class 28 Co-Bo. The month also saw a change in manufacturer for prototype DP2. Heljan announced that it would be producing the model and Dapol subsequently stepped back from its project to avoid repetition of the model. However, all was not lost for Dapol as the manufacturer revealed that it would be producing a brand new model of the 'Western' hydraulic for 'OO' and 'N' gauge together with a 'Hall' 4-6-0, Class 26 and Class 56 for 'N' gauge during 2011.

The feed of new releases was slower during January with Bachmann launching its Freightliner Powerhaul Class 70 for 'OO' while Hornby released its BR black GWR '28XX' and '2884' for 'OO' too.

February 2011

At Model Rail Scotland Hornby showcased the latest progress with liveried samples of its new Railroad model of 60163 Tornado and decorated samples of the 4-VEP EMU. The exhibition also saw Heljan debut decorated samples of its Class 23 'Baby Deltic' and the final pre-production sample of D0260 Lion.

New releases concentrated fully on reliveries of existing models with a new version of the Bachmann 'N' gauge Class 37/0 in BR green arriving together new Class 86s from Dapol for 'N' too. Other highlights included a Railway Technical Centre liveried Class 24 from Modelzone in 'N' plus a ScotRail Class 150/2 limited edition from Harburn Hobbies.

Above: Hornby issued its first all new Railroad model in the shape of new 'A1' 60163 Tornado.

Below: Bachmann brought the story right up to date with a new model of the Freightliner Class 70.

Left: Golden Age Models wowed the market with its premium model of the Gresley 'A4' 4-6-2.

March 2011

The third month of 2011 began with
Bachmann's annual catalogue launch
which saw the company reveal plans
for a GWR 'Dukedog' 4-4-0, SECR
Wainwright 'C' class 0-6-0, Class 419
Motor Luggage Van and LMS Porthole
stock in 'OO' gauge.

However, in 'N' gauge Bachmann
announced plans for nine new
locomotives covering the Peppercorn
'A1' 4-6-2, BR '5MT' 4-6-0, 'WD' 2-8-0,
Gresley 'J39' 0-6-0, Class 20, original
condition Class 08 diesel

shunter, Class 350 Desiro EMU, Class
411 4-CEP EMU and Blue Pullman
DEMU together with a selection of new
wagons and coaches.

Rail Exclusive began is journey to
produce a remastered Class 33/0 for
'OO' gauge by announcing its project
with Heljan too.

New releases were topped by Heljan's
BRCW prototype D0260 *Lion* and the
promised new Class 43 HST power cars
as book sets for 'N' gauge from Dapol.
Bachmann's Class 37/0 also returned
with upgrades to its body tooling and a
21-pin decoder chassis.

April 2011

In the news was Kernow Model Rail
Centre as the shop revealed the first
pre-production sample of its JIA china
clay bogie wagon while Hatton's showed
the final liveried samples of its Class 28
Co-Bo in BR green with full yellow ends.
Realtrack Models revealed the first pre-
production sample of its Class 143 DMU
while Dapol revealed the latest CAD/
CAM drawings for its all new 'N' gauge
Class 56.

New releases were headed by
Hornby's new RailMaster computer
control software which was designed to
operate with the Elite DCC controller.
Joining this new

development was the OTA timber wagon from Hornby, a new EMU/DMU chassis from Replica Railways and the latest version of the Warship hydraulic from Bachmann.

May 2011

It was new models galore in May with Kernow Model Rail Centre showing the first liveried samples of its Beattie Well Tank and Bachmann debuting the first pre-production engineering prototype of its Midland '3F' 0-6-0. The National Railway Museum also commissioned two limited edition models of Gresley 'A3' 4472 *Flying Scotsman* to mark its return to steam – albeit briefly due to cracks discovered in the frames.

New releases featured Hornby's Railroad model of 60163 *Tornado* and Bachmann's BR 2-EPB in 'OO' gauge plus Heljan's latest 'O' gauge model in the shape of the

Class 26 Bo-Bo. Other releases included a weathered version of the 'K3' 2-6-0 from Bachmann in 'OO' and new identities for the GWR pannier.

Contemporary wagons were also in vogue with Bachmann releasing its FNA nuclear flask wagon and the KFA container flat arrived from Hornby too.

June 2011

June marked the 50th issue of *Hornby Magazine* also saw the magazine announce and release its latest limited edition locomotive – a Bachmann Class 37/0 in BR green with a weathered finish as D6711. TMC also hit the news by commissioning a BR Mk 1 horsebox from Bachmann

together with new buildings. Bachmann released the first images of its pre-production Derby Lightweight DMU for 'OO' together with images of its 4-CEP and Class 350 for 'N' gauge. Meanwhile Dapol showed the latest development on its Class 52 Western for 'OO' with the CAD/CAM and laser scan drawings.

Dapol released its GWR 'Hall' 4-6-0 in 'N' gauge while OO Works launched its Midland '2F' 0-6-0 and Model Rail its Sentinel

Above: Bachmann and Dapol went head to head on the Thompson 'B1' in 'N' gauge. This is the Bachmann model.

Below: Hornby's delayed 4-VEP third-rail EMU touched down in July 2011.

Top Right: In 'O' gauge the Class 33 was one of three new offerings from Heljan during 2010/2011.

Second from top: Heljan's new 'O' gauge 'Deltic' arrive in the UK at the end of August 2011.

Second from bottom: Hattons/Heljan debuted the final versions of the Co-Bo in July 2011.

Bottom: Bachmann continued work on its 'N' gauge Class 101 to produce this attractive model.

4wVBT. Other highlights included a Crimson lake liveried 'Crab' 2-6-0 from Bachmann and a new sound fitted Gresley 'A4' from Hornby in the form of 60018 *Sparrow Hawk* in BR lined blue.

July 2011

The seventh month of the year saw one of the biggest announcements of the year as Hatton's revealed that it would be working with Heljan to produce an 'OO' gauge ready-to-run model of the LMS Beyer Garratt 2-6-0+0-6-2 for release in December 2012.

The annual Bachmann open day saw the manufacturer show the latest progress on its 'OO' and 'N' gauge ranges with pre-production samples of the Class 85 overhead electric making their debut together with the GWR ROD '3000' 2-8-0, Derby Lightweight DMU and OTA timber wagon in 'OO'. Decorated samples of the Midland '3F' and Class 105 power twin were also displayed together with the new DCC ready chassis for the 'A4' and 'B1' models.

In 'N' gauge the first pre-production sample of the BR '5MT' stole the show together with decorated samples of the Peppercorn 'A1' 4-6-2, new Mk 1 coaches and wagons.

Four brand new models made their debut in July with Hornby launching its 4-VEP third-rail EMU in BR rail blue, Bachmann its Network Rail MPV - both DCC ready and DCC fitted - and Hattons its second commissioned model from Heljan in the Class 28 Co-Bo in 'OO'. Plus the new Class 101 DMU in 'N' gauge arrived form Bachmann's Graham Farish brand. Hornby's new GWR Horsebox also arrived too offering a new steam era wagon from the manufacturer.

August 2011

During the final month of this review Hornby showed the first decorated samples of its new Thompson 'B1' 4-6-0 and Gresley suburban coaches while Bachmann also issued the first images of the Class 419 MLV. Heljan revealed the first pre-production model of DP2 and Dapol showcased its MRA side tipping ballast wagon sets. Kernow Model Rail Centre also approved all its livery samples for the Beattie '0298' allowing full production to commence.

New releases featured two impressive, but completely different models in the form of Kernow Model Rail Centre's Southern Railway liveried Beattie '0298' for 'OO' and Heljan's new 'O' gauge

ready-to-run model of the English Electric Class 55 'Deltic'. Other releases included Hornby's new BR 20ton brake van and BR 27ton tippler.

Hornby Magazine's opinion

With so many new releases and announcements it is, at times, becoming difficult to keep up with the range of models coming on stream. However, this is a great sign that this hobby is still growing and, perhaps most importantly, that we, as the modellers, are prepared to support the manufacturers in their ventures. The growth of the commission market continues to expand the horizons and locomotives which were once thought to be the preserve of kit manufacturers are now becoming commonplace as ready-to-run models. This does have an effect in the kit sector though, as it is becoming increasingly difficult to find subjects which won't become a ready-to-run production.

As a hobby railway modelling continues to grow and generate interest. We've said it before, but every month it becomes more and more exciting as new ventures are announced, detail standards are improved and new technology comes forward. Really, we couldn't ask for more! Roll on 2012…

Ballasting
and contours

The next two components of our layout project are to lay the ballast and create a secondary foundation – the scenic contours. **Mike Wild** describes how this can be achieved using simple techniques and materials.

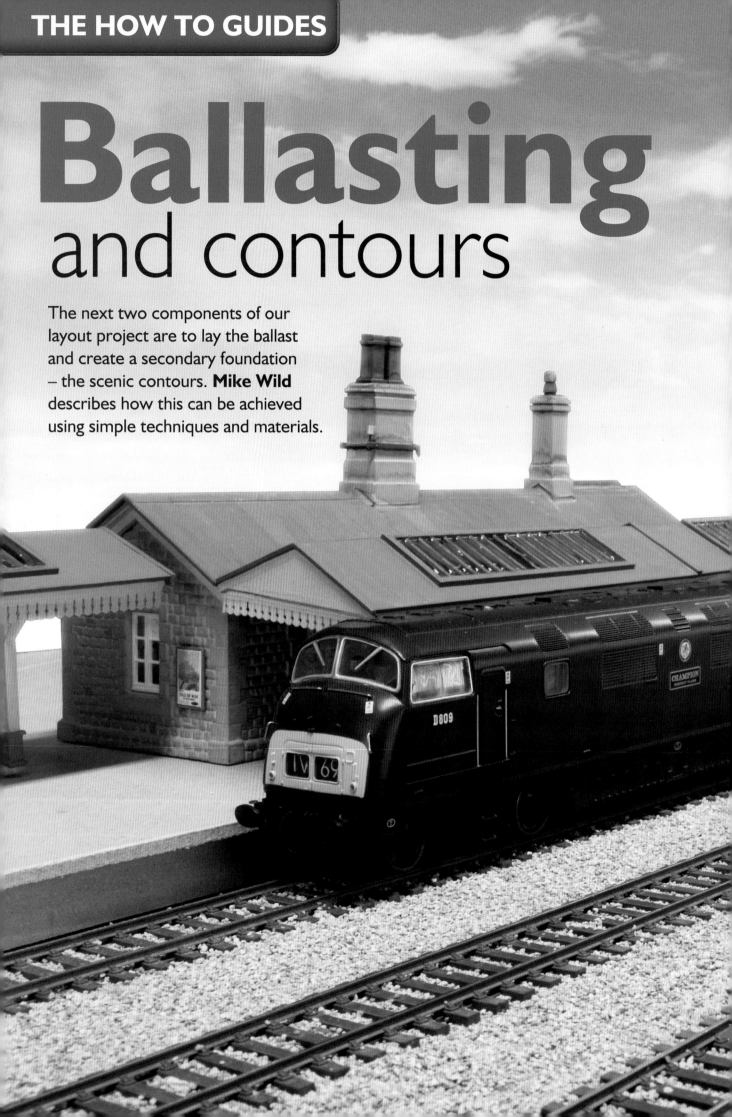

There is no point making things complicated. We don't build model railways to be entangled in difficulty, finding solutions to awkward problems – that can be reserved for the workday.

Many of the techniques that we use at *Hornby Magazine* HQ for layout construction are chosen for speed, durability and simplicity. Due to the timescales we work to on our projects we don't physically have the time to work slowly – a build has to move forward as quickly as possible and this, we hope, can help you too.

With the baseboards built and the track laid, including the electric connections for the control panel, the next most important task is ballast. In the real world this forms an integral part of railway construction holding the track in place and providing necessary

drainage too. In model terms ballast does neither of these things. Its sole purpose is to look like ballast!

There are many choices when it comes to ballast. There are ballast mats and pre-ballasted foam inserts and while this may tick one box as they are very simple and quick to use, in our view there is nothing to rival loose ballasting a model railway.

Loose ballasting isn't quite what it seems. The ballast is applied loose, but it isn't left that way. It has to be fixed in place and to do that a 50:50 mixture of PVA glue and water with a couple of drops of washing up liquid to remove the surface tension from the mixture and aid its flow through the ballast is ideal.

Back to the ballast. There are many products to choose from and colours too. Our preference is to use two

different grades and at least three harmonious colours to create our ballast. For St Stephens Road we used a combination of Woodland Scenics medium grade blended grey, fine grade blended grey and medium grade buff ballast. These three colours work well together, but also remove the uniformity of a single colour ballast.

We mix these together in a large tub, although the ratio of each colour isn't set – it is mixed till we feel it looks right. We then spread the ballast over the track loose with by picking it up between our fingers or tapping it out of the tub. The former method is much neater, but either way it will need brushing into place before the glue is applied.

The Step by Step guide with this feature illustrates how we went above ballasting St Stephens Road.

A 'Warship' enters the newly installed platform at St Stephens Road.

Above: A Bachmann 'Hall' 4-6-0 leads a passenger train along the newly ballasted track.

Right: A GWR 2-6-2T leads a goods through the newly formed cutting. The top layer of material is Woodland Scenics plaster cloth.

Scenic formwork

Unless you are modeling the flatlands of the fens, chances are you will want to add some relief to your layout. If you wanted the track to be higher than the scenery – on an embankment for example – then a completely different design of baseboard would be required

such as an open frame or L girder design.

However, for St Stephens Road we are using solid top baseboards so for the scenery the only way is up. This is another area where we have honed our techniques and while there is nothing revolutionary about them, they work.

The basis for this project is a couple of sheets of 50mm thick polystyrene insulation and a couple of offcuts of 25mm think polystyrene packing sheets. This material is easy to cut and shape to create hillsides, cuttings and any raised ground. It is also strong enough to create the road bridges which reside on

STEP 1: The first stage in loose ballasting after mixing grades and colours is to lay the ballast over the track. This is the single track main line leading to the fiddle yard. The ballast was laid by hand.

STEP 2: The next stage is to brush the ballast into position between the sleepers and either side to create a neat effect which is then ready to be glued in place.

STEP 3: To avoid point blades becoming stuck or electrically isolated during the glue stage add a few drops of locomotive oil between the blades and on all the moving parts. The glue will not stick to the oil and saves much cleaning up after the next stage.

STEP 4: To prepare the ballast for the PVA/water mix it needs to be wetted first so that the glue flows more easily into the ballast. This also reduces the chance of ballast moving during the gluing process. To wet the ballast we use a water mister available from garden centres.

STEP 5: A 50:50 mixture of PVA glue and water is mixed up in an old washing up liquid bottle with a couple of drops of washing up liquid added to remove surface tension from the mixture and aid its flow through the ballast. The glue can then be poured onto the wetted ballast from the bottle.

STEP 6: At this point the ballasting process is complete apart from being left overnight to set. It will look messy when the glue is still wet, but in the morning it should look almost the same as before the glue was applied.

A Bachmann 'Warship' enters the scenic section through the newly formed cutting.

the layout making it highly versatile.

The polystyrene base is overlaid with Woodland Scenics plaster cloth which is cloth embedded with plaster. This is wetted then laid over the scenic formwork before being smoothed out – the plaster creating a solid surface, particularly once two or three layers are applied.

At this stage the layout is almost ready for scenic work to start, but first all of the plaster covered cuttings and hillsides need a coat of brown paint to act as a base. Here it is very simple poster paint brushed on.

A platform in 30 minutes

The method of platform construction follows an idea we had for *Hornby Magazine's* Layout in a Weekend challenge which took place at Hornby Magazine LIVE! in Hartlepool in July 2011. For this project we needed something quick, robust and simple to assemble so we hit upon the idea of using 12mm MDF for the base overlaid with 3.5mm hardboard to create the top surface.

As St Stephens Road has a curved island platform with two faces it was a little more complex to make than the Layout in a Weekend projects straight platforms, but with a little thought and

STEP-BY-STEP BUILDING A PLATFORM BASE FROM WOOD

STEP 1: To create the double faced curved platform for this layout we needed to produce a template first. Sheets of A4 paper were taped together then cut roughly to shape so that they would fit between the two platform tracks.

STEP 2: With this template held in place on the baseboard with masking tape, a pen was held against the end of coach and moved through the platform to mark the position of the inside curve. Use the longest coach you will be operating to ensure adequate clearance for all vehicles.

STEP 3: To mark the outside curve of the platform the pen now needs to be positioned in the centre of the longest coach for the layout and the process repeated. This template is then used to mark up the timber sheets to make the platform.

planning it took just 30 minutes to cut and assemble the basics.

Firstly sheets of A4 paper were laid over the platform area and taped together with masking tape. The edge of the cork base was then marked on this and a rough template was cut out and laid back in place. With this taped to the baseboard so it couldn't move a pen was held against the end of a Mk I coach, the longest to operate on St Stephens -

you should always use the longest coach on your layout for this marking stage – to mark the curve of the Southern Region platform while to mark the Western Region side the pen was held in the middle. In each case the pen is held where the coaches swing is greatest.

The template was then cut out again with scissors before being transferred onto the timber. For the MDF base this was narrowed by 3mm to create

an overhang by reducing the width by 1.5mm on each side. The hardboard top used the full width of the template. The hardboard top was also shaped to create an entrance area for road traffic at the station forecourt.

With all this progressed St Stephens Road is ready for scenic treatment where it will begin to represent a miniature world through the addition of grass trees and more.

A '4575' 2-6-2T passes under the road bridge which was the first part of the scenic structure to be installed.

STEP 4: The base of the platform is 12mm MDF. It has been cut 3mm narrower than the hardboard top to create an overhang for the top surface.

STEP 5: This is the hardboard top laid in place for checking of clearances before final fitting. The MDF was also trimmed back 70mm at each end to create the slope for the platform ends.

STEP 6: A GWR pannier tank sits in the centre road with the newly installed platform now awaiting a plasticard stone face and painting of the surface.

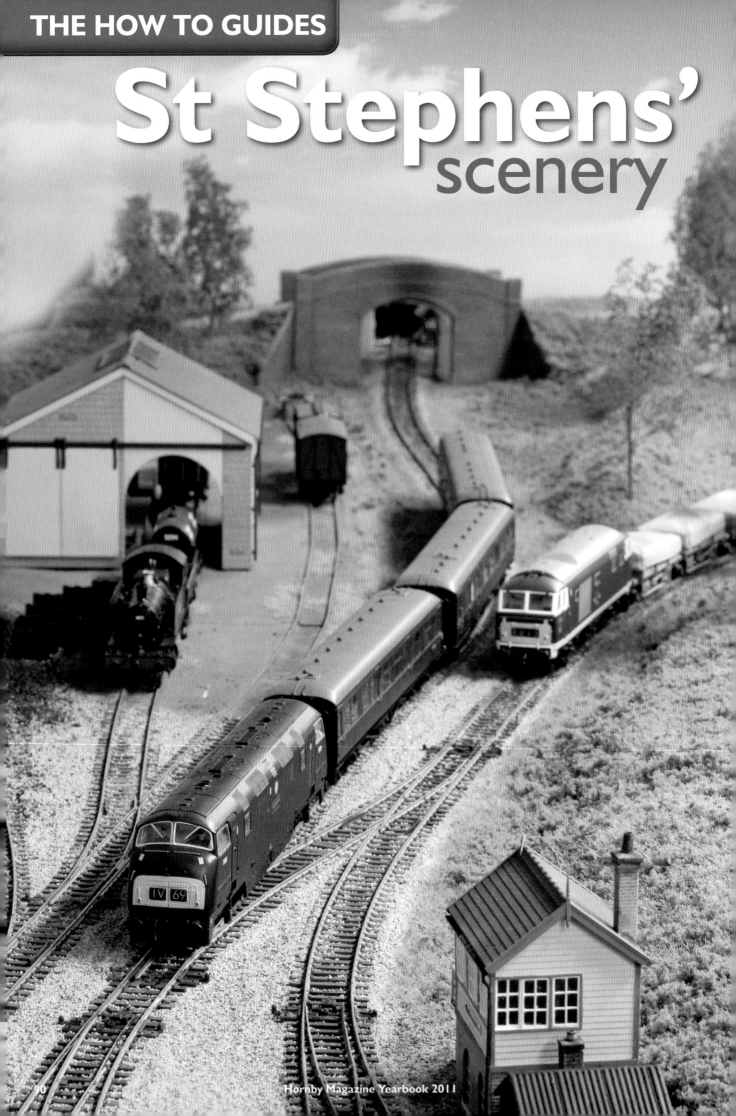

IV 69

Scenery transforms a model railway from its basic concept to a miniature world. **Mike Wild** explains how St Stephens Road has been treated to create rich textures with a realistic finish.

Like so many aspects of model railway construction scenic ground cover is often seen as a black art, but in this feature we'll show that with a few simple techniques and the right products you too can go about refreshing or building your scenery to a similar standard.

There are three key elements which make the difference on a scenic model railway – layered textures, blending and the bedding of buildings. Starting with the latter buildings will always look out of place if they are simply placed on top of ground cover. Rough terrain doesn't fit well with the straight edges of a building, but there are ways and means of setting buildings into their surrounds which only takes a little thought and planning.

For starters we'll look at the signalbox and platelayers hut which sit alongside the junction for the Western and Southern lines. It would be very easy to create a ballast base for these two structures and then simply place them on top. They would look just as good externally, but the bottom of each building wouldn't sit flat with the ballast below which would make them look uneasy to the eye. The simple way around this is to glue the buildings down first then add loose ballast around their footings, gluing it in place with a 50:50 ratio of PVA and water applied with a pipette. This sets them in place and there will be no chance of rough

edges or a rocky base to the two structures.

The goods shed on St Stephens Road requires a slightly different technique. The air dry clay base under the building is uneven and so the goods shed won't sit entirely flush with the base all the way around. This time additional scenic treatment is needed to bed the building in which comes in the form of Woodland Scenics coarse turfs which can be carefully glued around the base of the building as required, but not all the way round – this would potentially look too uniform - to bed it into its surroundings.

Ground cover

Single layers of ground cover rarely produce a good looking and textured finish for a model railway, so all of *Hornby Magazine's* layouts – St Stephens Road is no exception – use a layer technique which sees the ground cover build up in stages.

Producing ground cover this way takes a little planning and forethought. Roads need to be painted first and for this we use a light grey emulsion paint mixed with a small amount of Woodland Scenics fine ballast to create a textured paint. This is then brushed onto the road surfaces where required using either two or three coats depending upon coverage. We also paint the roads wider than necessary as this allows them to be blended in at the next stage.

Because all the ballasting has already been completed on the layout we have all the basics in place and it is now time to start adding the first layer of ground cover over the scenic formwork. This begins with a coat of neat PVA glue applied with a paint brush. Work in 1ft or 2ft square areas to avoid the glue going off too quickly.

The first layer of ground cover consists of a dusting of Woodland Scenics fine blended turf sprinkled over the glue from two or three feet above for an even finish. With this done we use a Noch Grasmaster to apply a layer of static grass. This device applies a static charge to the grass fibres – MiniNatur autumn and winter fibres in 4.5mm and 6.5mm lengths in this case – which makes them stand on end. Another dusting of Woodland Scenics fine blended green turf is then added on top.

Mixing different hues of green together enhances the finished result as there are always a number of different greens in grass depending on the time of year, time of day and the angle of the light.

A 'Warship' approaches St Stephens Road on the Western Region branch while a 'Hymek' (a rare visitor to Cornwall) waits on the joint Western and Southern line with a china clay train. Signals had still to be added at this stage of the project together with a host of detailing.

STEP-BY-STEP — ADDING TEXTURE AND COLOUR TO ST STEPHENS ROAD

STEP 1: Scenery works best when built up in layers. The first to be applied were the ballast around the track, air dry clay base for the goods yard and the textured paint finish for the road. The latter is created using Woodland Scenics fine grey blended ballast mixed with a light grey emulsion paint.

STEP 2: To begin adding ground cover a neat layer of PVA glue was brushed over each area which required grass coverage.

STEP 3: A dusting of Woodland Scenics fine blended green turf was then added to the glue.

STEP 4: Using a Noch Grasmaster MiniNatur autumn and winter grass fibres were then applied over the blended turf and glue.

STEP 5: To add a little depth to this first layer of grass another dusting of blended green turf was added into the static grass.

A 'Hymek' enters St Stephens Road with a china clay train. Grass and trees have been added leaving the track requiring weathering to complete this area.

We also avoid harsh greens – often marketed as spring or summer – as these tend to be a little too vivid for a model railway when colour scaling is taken into account.

Adding texture

This first layer is all well and good, but it will still leave a lot of showthrough from the formwork below. Before proceeding to the second layer it is worth running a vacuum cleaner over the areas of grass to remove any loose material which will impact on the result of the next stage.

The second layer follows broadly the same pattern as the first. However, rather than neat PVA, a 75:25 mixture of PVA and water is applied with a brush over the first layer of grass. This flows into the first layer and won't squash it down. More blended turf can then be sprinkled over the wet glue followed by another treatment with static grass using a mixture of winter and autumn colour grasses in this case.

However, this isn't the final part of the process. To really bring the ground cover to life we use a mixture of Woodland Scenics coarse turfs in light green and olive green together with more of Woodland Scenics fine blended turf and flowering foliage. This is all applied loose to the layout and rubbed into position working with the coarse and fine turfs initially. Using a matt varnish aerosol – we find Railmatch matt varnish to be the most suitable, particularly for its spray pressure – the coarse and fine turfs can then be fixed in position by spraying varnish over them. Start by applying the varnish from around 2ft above the layout to begin fixing it in place, then move in

STEP-BY-STEP ADDING TEXTURE AND COLOUR TO ST STEPHENS ROAD

STEP 6: At this point the first layers looks smart, but it is still thin in places and a little too uniform.

STEP 7: A second coat of PVA glue – this time diluted with water to a 75:25 ratio of glue to water – is brushed over the first layer of grass.

STEP 8: Woodland Scenics fine blended green turf is again sprinkled into the wet glue.

STEP 9: A further layer of static grass can now be added onto the wet glue giving greater depth and texture to the scenery.

STEP 10: To enhance the goods yard small areas were treated with dilute PVA glue followed by a dusting of fine blended turf and more static grass through the Noch Grasmaster. It looks messy in this view, but this all changes with cleaning up with a vacuum cleaner.

closer once it begins to take hold.

While the varnish is still wet further colours and textures can be worked in on top. This is were a pinch of fine blended turf or a sprinkle of flowering foliage can really add something to the overall look as by using just the coloured flock from the latter can create the effect of small flowers growing through the bushes – the yellow, for example, looks like buttercups and the purple could be representative of berries.

Going the extra mile

This is all the start of the process as the layout is now ready to be taken a stage further. It will still look bare, because what it lacks is trees and detailing such as bushes and fencing.

To make the trees for St Stephens Road we used a box of seamoss which is available from International Models. This can be used in large pieces to make big trees, or split into small sections to make small trees and bushes. To turn the raw material into trees it is sprayed with a brown paint from an aerosol then covered with Woodland Scenics fine blended green turf. This produces a good looking tree for minimal cost and it can be a very quick process too. All of the trees on this layout took a little over an hour to make.

Bushes and hedge rows are created in a similar fashion. The base medium is Woodland Scenic polyfibre. This is teased out to create long thin strips or small bushes then sprayed with brown spray paint before being rolled in more Woodland Scenics fine blended green turf to create the finished effect.

Other areas requiring attention include the platform. The surface for this was painted with grey emulsion paint and, while still wet, Woodland Scenics fine blended grey ballast was then sprinkled at random over the paint to give the effect of loose chippings on the platform surface and also a little extra colour. To add more to this, and without loosing the colour and texture of the first layer, the platform surface was blown over with matt varnish and a few extra pinches of fine mixed grey ballast added to it.

With all this done it takes us to the point where the buildings are bedded in and all the scenic ground cover is complete. However, naturally we will want more detail for the layout and we'll explain how we developed this layout further on pages 100-105.

For now the following Step by Step guide will show more of what we did with St Stephens Road's scenery.

USEFUL LINKS

| Woodland Scenics | www.bachmann.co.uk |
| International Models | www.internationalmodels.net |

A 'Small Prairie' enters the scenic section of St Stephens Road through the newly created scenic textures.

STEP 11: After cleaning off the excess material with a vacuum cleaner it leaves a handful of grass tufts between and around the track enhancing the appearance of the goods yard.

STEP 12: The platform surface is created by painting it with grey emulsion paint then adding fine blended grey ballast on top of the wet glue to give it greater texture. Platform walls are made from strips of Wills coarse stone sheets which are cut to size and glued in place with multi-purpose glue.

STEP 13: The final covering of grass texture is achieved by using coarse turfs, fine turfs and flowering foliage – all from Woodland Scenics. This is applied loose to the grass areas before being fixed in place with Railmatch matt varnish from an aerosol spray can.

STEP 14: To bed the two houses into their surroundings and to give them neat trimmed grass gardens PVA was brushed around the grey painted base areas and covered with Woodland Scenics fine blended green turf. A second layer was added by covering the first layer with dilute PVA glue after it had dried.

STEP 15: The final stage in this part of the process is to begin adding trees and bushes. All of the trees in this view are made from seamoss which is sprayed brown then covered with fine blended green turf.

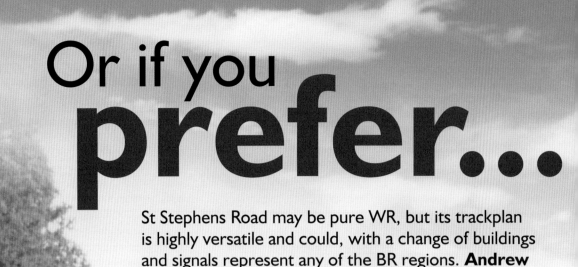

Or if you prefer...

St Stephens Road may be pure WR, but its trackplan is highly versatile and could, with a change of buildings and signals represent any of the BR regions. **Andrew Roden** presents three very different scenarios for steam and diesel modellers. *Photography, Mike Wild.*

Having covered three of the former 'Big Four' railways' territories in previous *Hornby Magazine* project layouts, opting for a Great Western Railway/Western Region setting was an easy choice to make for St Stephens Road. With its distinctive architecture and lower quadrant semaphore signals - not to mention the distinctive GWR based steam fleet and hydraulic diesels - the layout oozes WR atmosphere, but what if your interests lie elsewhere?

Buildings and signals aside, there's little in the trackplan of St Stephens Road which singles it out as having any particular origin, and that means that the concept can be used for a whole range of scenarios for steam and diesel modellers from the 1950s to the present day. We picked three options which we found particularly attractive, and to give an idea of what they might look like, we used other *Hornby Magazine* layouts as well as St Stephens Road.

SCENARIO 1

St Stephens in blue

LOCATION/PERIOD

British Rail Western Region, 1970s/80s

The Western Region was the first to eliminate steam operation, by the end of 1965, but there was plenty to attract diesel enthusiasts, which is why our first scenario uses St Stephens Road, transported 10 years or so into the future.

One of the nice things about Cornish railways of the 1970s and early 1980s was that the routes hadn't been rationalised into what are today, effectively single track sidings - and that provides plenty of scope for operating variety.

You could easily transpose the layout into the 1970s by changing the station signage and making it look a little more neglected, but otherwise it would have been very similar to the 1950s. Where it gets particularly interesting, though, is in the sheer variety of traction. Although by the mid 1970s the 'Warship' diesel-hydraulics had all gone, you could justify a Class 52 'Western' on freight duties (passenger trains would have been in the hands of DMUs or diesel-electric locomotives except on very rare occasions) and a heavily weathered Class 08 shunter could haul a rake of china clay 'hood' wagons to St Stephens Road for a main line locomotive to take onwards. One class which was extremely rare in Cornwall was the Class 35 'Hymek'.

Throughout the 1970s and early 1980s, Class 25s were extensively used

Converting St Stephens Road to a 1970s theme would be a simple process and offer a new lease of operation to the layout. A BR blue liveried Class 37 enters the loops at the station with a rake of china clay hoods destined for the clay dries.

on freight work, supplemented by Class 37s from around 1978 and Class 46s on occasion. Class 47s became gradually more popular through the 1970s and 1980s too. Whether the goods yard would have survived is a good question. By the early 1980s the odds are that it would have been in terminal decline, but this provides the opportunity to enhance the china clay operation by running trip freights to the yard where longer block trains could be formed for onward movement.

When it comes to passenger workings, a decision needs to be taken on whether the branch should retain its service, become freight only - or even be transformed into a heritage railway like the Bodmin and Wenford. Assuming that the whole spectrum of services is going to be modelled, a Class 108 DMU would be perfect for the branch and local passenger services, but with a little imagination we can justify locomotive hauled expresses to London, as Class 50s hauled a portion of the 'Cornish Riviera' over the Falmouth branch from 1975 until 1979. Hornby's sublime 'OO' gauge model and three or four air-conditioned

Mk 2s really wouldn't look out of place at St Stephens Road at all, and would provide some distinct variety.

Bringing the operational period for St Stephens Road forward is an easy and attractive way of enhancing the layout's scope, and because so little infrastructure has changed, with a little effort you might even be able to bring it right up to date. If you modelled the station in 2011, the goods yard would

have to go - if not replaced by a car park, then perhaps by a supermarket - and the station building might now be in private hands. That might, in turn, allow you to model a camping coach such as those at St Germans, which have been converted into luxury holiday accommodation. Passenger services would be provided by a Class 150 or Class 153 DMU, but although you could run a High Speed Train on a summer Saturday service

from London, space constraints might lead you to prefer a Class 220 Voyager instead. China clay is still carried, so some CDA wagons and a Class 66 could cater for that, while converting the branch to a heritage railway would remain an option too.

Steam's Indian Summer

LOCATION/PERIOD

British Railways London Midland Region, 1950s

If there's one thing which the steam railway absolutely depended on, it was coal. Not only did the black gold fuel the locomotives; it also provided a huge chunk of revenue. For our second scenario, we've focussed firmly on the mid 1950s when steam still firmly held sway, and only the occasional diesel shunter or DMU disturbed the scene.

By doing a straight swap of china clay for coal, St Stephens Road could easily represent a station in the East Midlands or South Yorkshire coalfield on a secondary route - and the operating potential is epic. The heavy freight traffic would provide a plethora of choices for locomotives, from '3F' and '4F' 0-6-0s to 'Super D' 0-8-0s, '8F' and 'WD' 2-8-0s and even, perhaps, '9F' 2-10-0s. Being firmly in ex-Midland Railway territory, you could expect to see a '2P' or '4P' 4-4-0 on local passenger duties, as well as 'Black Fives' and British Railways '4MT' 2-6-0s and '5MT' 4-6-0s. To truly set the scene, a 'Jinty' 0-6-0T shunting the yard, and perhaps one of the delightful Ivatt '2MT' 2-6-2Ts would provide ample variation. Completists could acquire a 'Hunslet' 0-6-0ST in National Coal Board colours and occasionally run that to the junction too, or perhaps a more specialist industrial type - the scope there is vast.

Coaching stock would invariably be ex-LMS Stanier designs, but with such a complex web of lines in the East Midlands/South Yorkshire it would be easy to justify some ex-LNER Gresley coaches too. LNER locomotives such as 'B1' 4-6-0s, or 'O4' 2-8-0s could be incorporated without too much fuss, while modellers wanting to realistically run express passenger locomotives could claim that the route is being used for diversions. This opens up the prospect of ex-LMS 'Jubilee' and 'Patriot' 4-6-0s, as well as ex-LNER 'A3' 4-6-2s and 'V2' 2-6-2s appearing on the line.

As far as diesels are concerned, a Class 08 shunter would be the only realistic candidate for a pre-1955 scenario, while towards the ends of the 1950s it becomes possible to incorporate early main line designs such as Class 20s and 24s, though these would be in a distinct minority.

Although the predominant freight on the branch line would be coal, the need for general traffic would offer plenty of variety elsewhere, and with British Railways wagons of the period being increasingly well catered for off the shelf, a really representative scene would be fairly straightforward to create.

We debated long and hard during the planning process whether to do just this scenario: in terms of variety of traction and operation the setting is compelling, and in 'OO' scale (and to a lesser extent, 'N'), the range of readily available locomotives, carriages and wagons is remarkably comprehensive.

Left: With a change of buildings and signals the trackplan for St Stephens Road could be adapted to suit the London Midland Region where goods traffic was king. Offering an impression of how it might look a Stanier '8F' passes through Bolsover with a long goods.

Below: If the Southern Region is your area of interest, then now is a good time to consider it as a potential layout subject with the recent release of a 4-CEP and 2-EPB from Bachmann.

Above: **The Scottish Highlands have long been a popular subject with modellers and the plan for St Stephens could be built with a selection of suitable buildings to represent the area. A BRCW Type 2 departs Berrybridge with a short passenger working.**

Right: **A Class 108 DMU approaches Berrybridge. DMUs can provide short but complete trains to the compact layout builder.**

The classic Scottish junction station

LOCATION/PERIOD

British Railways Scottish Region, 1960s

One of the things Scotland's railways had in common with those of the South West were lengthy single track secondary routes with bustling junction stations, and St Stephens Road could easily be sited somewhere like the Moray coast, which despite being in the Highlands, is fairly flat farming country.

The multitude of different pre-grouping steam classes still in operation in the 1950s might make sourcing suitable off-the-shelf products tricky, but moving the period forward into the mid 1960s provides a wealth of opportunities for a transition era layout. The junction lends itself readily to a DMU service, and freight traffic could be based around grain for a whisky maltings, such as those at Roseisle or Burghead, which were reached by a branch off the Inverness-Aberdeen line.

In terms of locomotives, you could justify a 'Black Five' 4-6-0, and you can even stretch the case a little to include an 'A4' 4-6-2, perhaps working a railtour rather than the Edinburgh-Aberdeen duties they finished their careers on. The bulk of trains need to be hauled by diesels, however, with classes 25/26/27 predominating on this secondary route. Coaching stock by the 1960s would have been mostly Mk 1s, with DMUs such as Class 101s working local services. With a mixture of types and short trains, a Scottish setting would suit St Stephens Road perfectly, and you could even stretch the time period without having to change much: substitute a Class 37 or 66 for the Type 2s, and a Class 156 or 158 for the Class 101, and you can model any period from the 1960s to the present day.

Whatever you decide to do, the trackplan for St Stephens Road offers a wealth of possibility for all sorts of exciting operations - the only challenge is deciding what you want to do most.

Above: A 'Warship' passes St Stephen's goods yard while a Class 08 shunts china clay wagons in the goods yard. This scene transport the layout forward to the early 1970s.

Developing
a model railway

The development of a model railway is a continuous process and one which can go on for as long as the builder is content. **Mike Wild** explains how the process of developing St Stephens Road began. *Photography, Mike Wild.*

In the scenery section of the St Stephens Road project we took the layout to the point where it looked like a railway set in the landscape, but equally it was missing all the vital details which take it to the next level. Detailing is all part of the model railway construction process. What we've done for this project is taken it to a point where it has detail, but equally there is still room for improvement

and further detailing in the future.

When adding more to a model railway it is easy to get carried away and go too far, cluttering the scene rather than enhancing. This is why we are comfortable with the way St Stephens Road looks in its 'finished' state as the layout isn't overdone, but leaves room for more to be added in the future.

During this process it is a good idea to step back every now and then and review how various scenes are coming together. It might be that after installing items such as signals a tree needs to be

repositioned or removed altogether or maybe the route of telegraph poles need to be changed to allow more trees to be planted. The same can be said for bushes. We added more to the layout during the detailing stage, but again we know there is room for more of this in the future.

Filling pockets

One of the more attractive features, we feel at least, is the pair of thatched cottages which sit slightly elevated above the level of the railway in one corner. When we started on this area we had a

WHAT WE USED

Product	Cat No.	Supplier
MiniNatur flowers (purple, red, white, orange)	Various	International Models
Polyfibre	FP178	Woodland Scenics
Lineside fencing	425	Ratio
GWR spear fencing	434	Ratio
Milk churns	R8678	Hornby
Platform trolley and sack barrows	Various	Dart Castings
Ground signals	465	Ratio
GWR lower quadrant stop signal	460	Ratio
GWR lower quadrant I bracket signal	469	Ratio
GWR/LMS joint loading gauge	411	Ratio
Boxes, kegs and pallets	Various	Base Toys
Road vehicles	Various	Oxford Diecast
Road vehicles	Various	Base Toys

vision of what we wanted to achieve. The aim was to create a well tended garden with flowers and vegetable plot with the next door garden being less well tended with a more random approach to its appearance.

Partially this has been done through differing styles of hedge. The well tended garden has a richer and tidier hedge while the 'developing' garden has a rougher hedge with branches growing out of the top of it. In the garden of the latter we've also built a small pile of logs to suggest

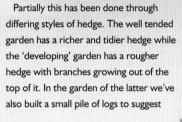

that the owners are making progress with clearing the garden. A selection of vegetables from a Noch laser cut pack enhance the scene.

The well tended garden features a range of Noch laser cut items including vegetables, wooden runners for peas and MiniNatur flowers all adding to the well tended feel of the scene.

Other areas requiring colour and detail were the grassed banks around the station. The main feature of these is either a hedge row made from teased out polyfibre, spray painted brown and covered with fine blended green turf from Woodland Scenics or Ratio lineside fencing. The latter is available in either white or black plastic, but for this layout is has been spray painted with Humbrol No. 29 acrylic. To give the fencing a

 Top: A 'Hymek' draws its reformed pick up goods into the goods loops as a 'Warship' enters on the main line. The station lamp is from DCC Concepts.

 Above: A GWR/AEC railcar enters St Stephens between a pair of GWR lower quadrant signals. The Ratio kits for the signals come with pre-painted arms and opaque lenses.

Left: A BR green 'Warship' enters St Stephens Road and passes the stop signal controlling departures in the opposite direction. Other features include a Peco rail built buffer stop, MiniNatur flowers and a Peco road over rail bridge.

Top: A Bachmann 'Hall' 4-6-0 leads a rake of Hornby Hawksworth coaches along the GWR route towards St Stephens.

Top right: The goods yard has been populated with an array of pallets, boxes and kegs from Base Toys together with a BD container placed adjacent to the loading dock and crane. The three arm bracket signal can be seen behind the Collett '2251'.

Right: A polyfibre hedge separates the fields from the railway as a 'Warship' powers up to draw a 'summer Saturday' express through the station.

Bottom right: A pannier draws a pair of 16ton mineral wagons forward for the coal bunker.

slightly aged look a handful of planks have been broken at one end and bent down or cut out altogether.

To add a little colour to the hedge and fence rows small pieces of seamoss have been painted brown and covered with more fine blended green turf so that they overhang the fence while in other areas MiniNatur flowers – using a selection of red, purple, white and orange – have been dotted around along the fence lines.

Detailing the railway

The major missing element from the railway were signals. Signals really make a difference whether they are operational or not and for St Stephens Road we used the Ratio square post GWR lower quadrants to fit in with the BR Western Region theme.

In total there are 10 signals on the layout together with four ground signals with eight being single arm stop signals, one bracket signal to control the junction from the Southern to the Western Region and one three arm bracket signal to

control trains approaching the station from the main line alongside the goods yard. Rather than mix two regions signaling designs for the Western and Southern routes we felt the layout would look more realistic with purely GWR pattern signalling – after all, they are all controlled from a GWR signalbox.

The eight stop signals were simple to construct as they don't even require painting. Each one has a pre-painted signal arm with opaque lenses and they are a joy to build. Similarly the double arm bracket signal is fairly straightforward to build, except for the operating mechanism which is a little more challenging.

The most difficult signal to build for St Stephens was the three arm bracket. This has been built by combining two twin arm bracket signal kits as Ratio doesn't produce a dedicated kit for this type of signal. The one concession with this signal is that the arms can currently only be operated by hand as adding the Ratio base design doesn't allow for three

arms to be operated independently.

Beyond the signals the railway also gained a GWR pattern loading gauge for the goods yard and a Wills coal bunker too. Adding to this is a small loading dock next to the goods shed with a Wills yard crane and a selection of boxes, pallets, kegs and a Conflat container on the yard floor.

The station

Naturally the station area is a prime candidate for detailing. Even with the station building and canopies installed it still looked somewhat bare, but this was soon corrected with a suitable selection of details.

First was a selection of benches. These aren't strictly GWR pattern, but the Peco station benches we used have been spray painted brown to match the station colour scheme and positioned both under the canopy and along the open part of the platform.

Another important addition was a set of station lamps. These are from DCC

8 Above left: **DCC** Concepts station lamps are simple to install and come with a light control board to manage the brightness of the lamps. The platform trolley and sack barrow are Dart Castings white metal models while the wicker baskets are from Hornby and the station bench from Peco.

9 Above right: Outside the station building a collection of empty milk churns wait to be loaded along with wicker baskets.

10 Left: The gardens of the two cottages have been given subtly different finishes. On the left the garden is well tended with a vegetable patch created using Noch laser cut minis and a row of roses growing alongside. The second garden by contrast is less well tended with a more ramshackle appearance.

St Stephen's Road

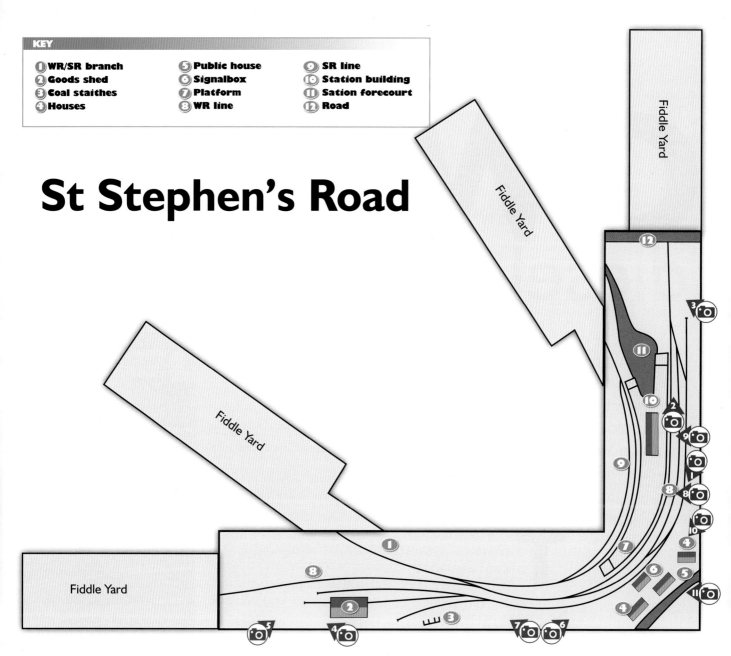

Fiddle Yard

Fiddle Yard

Fiddle Yard

Fiddle Yard

Concepts exquisite range of 4mm scale working gas lamps. They are pre-painted and assembled making their installation very simple. Each pack includes a light control circuit board which allows the colour and brightness of the lamps to be controlled from bright white to a dull yellow glow offering a realistic gas lamp effect.

With these added it was simply a case of raiding our 'bits box' to find a selection of milk churns, wicker baskets, platform trolleys and sack barrows plus a couple of trunks. These are from a range of sources including Dart Castings, Merit and Peco.

The future

No layout is ever finished and that is no more true than of St Stephens Road. Look carefully at these photographs and I'm you will spot the missing ingredient straight away – people. The layout is yet to be populated, but this will happen

gradually in the coming months.

Another major development under consideration is a brand new fiddle yard for the layout. While its multi-traverser fiddle yard arrangement works well in a home situation we have found it to be a little clumsy under exhibition conditions as it doesn't allow the most fluid change over of trains.

Having trialled the original fiddle yard plan for an operating session the plan as this Yearbook went to press was to create a continuous run for the layout which would effectively turn the layout into two separate circuits – one for the Western and one for the Southern.

The result of this will be that St Stephens will become a rather unusual shape – triangular! However, on paper it looks like it will be much more flexible for exhibition operations and also allow for some longer 'summer Saturday' trains to be incorporated into the roster transporting holiday makers to the

coastal terminus of the line.

No matter how well developed a model railway is there is always something new to add. Doubtless St Stephens locomotive and rolling stock fleet will continue to grow particularly with such attractive GWR locomotives as the 'Dukedog' from Bachmann on the cards for 2012.

Beyond this there is one further idea on the table – conversion to DCC. Having built and operated Bolsover – our BR Eastern Region layout – on the exhibition circuit with full DCC control and sound fitted locomotives the temptation of adding a sound chip to a 'Western' or 'Warship' and recreating the sound of a pair of twin Maybach engines drawing out of a station may prove too much to resist. Look out for future updates on St Stephens Road in *Hornby Magazine's* Staff Projects section.

For now though I'll let the photographs do the talking…

Left: Overlooking the two cottages which stand on one corner of the layout, the gardens, road and railway details are all plain to see. Note the GWR lower quadrant semaphores and loading gauge.

Above: The final trackplan for St Stephens Road. As drawn it would fit in a purpose built garden shed or part of a large garage.

The GWR's diesel pioneers

Diesel multiple units, or railcars, are largely thought of as a product of the 1950s Modernisation Plan, but in one area of the country at least by then diesels were already old news. **EVAN GREEN-HUGHES** looks at the Great Western Railway's fleet of railcars, which pre-date modernisation by some 20 years.

Throughout the early years of the 20th century British railway companies were facing steadily rising costs and declining revenue, particularly on their branch and secondary networks. Motor vehicles began to take a bigger share of the revenue, particularly in the years after the First World War when there were plenty of ex-army lorries and buses on the market which a potential operator could snap up at a bargain price. Crippling strikes across the railway network didn't help either.

Most railways began to explore ways of cutting costs and, naturally, much of the attention was focussed on the steam locomotive and its carriages. The conventional train had several disadvantages. It was costly to build, required a large number of people to run it and was cumbersome and inflexible, particularly when used on a short branch line. A large number of experiments took place with a view to cutting these costs with single coach self-contained steam railmotors being one solution, while another was to harness a conventional small locomotive to a coach which could be pushed or pulled as required.

During this period the internal combustion engine was developing rapidly to offer an alternative to steam and as early as 1903 railcars began to appear. The London Brighton and South Coast Railway had two four-wheelers, the Great Northern tried another on the Hatfield-Hertford route and the North Eastern had its bogie petrol-electrics, one of which survives today and is being restored to working order. The Great Western added a petrol-electric four-wheeler from British Thompson Houston in 1911, numbered 100, but this lasted only until 1919, mostly working on the Windsor branch. Generally speaking these early vehicles were not able to provide the required level of reliability and the experiments did not lead to widespread production.

Promising potential

However, by the early 1930s technology had advanced sufficiently for viable railcars to be constructed. The London and North Eastern Railway had a few diesel-electrics which worked alongside its Sentinel steam cars but these were still regarded as experimental vehicles so it was left to the Great Western Railway to introduce the UK's first fully successful internal combustion powered self-contained train.

The design of what was to become the first of the GWR's fleet of railcars originated not within the corridors of Swindon Works but at Hardy Motors of Southall (which had recently become part of AEC) where, in 1933, a railcar was designed around the AEC 130hp diesel engine. This railcar was quite unlike anything which had gone before, for early efforts had resembled either contemporary trams or garden sheds and later versions had more often than not resembled wooden boxes with windows fitted. This, on the other hand, was a stylish streamlined vehicle which was powered by the latest in road vehicle technology, adapted for railway use, and incorporated many of the mechanical features which were later to become so familiar on first generation diesel units.

Initially regarded as experimental the

chassis for what was to become railcar No 1 was assembled at the Hardy Motors plant and was then taken by road to the Park Royal coachworks where the body was constructed using traditional wooden frame methods. Once completed it was moved to the Commercial Motor Transport Exhibition at Olympia where it was reported that the Great Western Railway had purchased the vehicle and intended to use it on services between Slough and Reading. The vehicle was 62ft long and mounted on two four-wheeled bogies, but because it weighed less than 20 tons and was streamlined the 130hp engine could produce sufficient power for acceptable levels of speed and acceleration in service, with 60mph

Above: The clean lines of the GWR built diesel railcars are demonstrated to good effect in this view of W20, part of the first batch of Swindon built vehicles. In its last year of service, in 1962, it waits at Shrewsbury between duties, posing next to a Hymek Type 3 diesel-hydraulic. Colour Rail.

Left: Although the first railcars were designed for lightweight inter-city duties, they later became synonymous with cross-country routes such as that from Ruabon to Barmouth. W20 calls there on a Talyllyn Railway Preservation Society Railtour on September 25 1954. Colour Rail.

By now in the twilight of its career, W20 brings a splash of colour to Gloucester on May 27 1958. 'WD' 90188 would outlast the railcar by three years, being withdrawn in April 1965. Colour Rail.

being possible. A total of 69 people could be carried, it had a luggage compartment at one end, and the double-ended body was one of the first railway projects ever to benefit from design and testing using a wind tunnel. The power unit was mounted in the body but offset to one side and drove two of the axles via a flexible drive to the outside of the axles. An epicyclic bus-style gearbox was also used.

Warm reception

When the railcar entered service it was used on up to 16 workings a day, including on the Henley-on-Thames and Windsor branches and covered over 200 miles every day. It was well received by passengers, fast and reliable and returned more than seven miles per gallon. So good was the concept that this railcar ran continuously until 1955 without any form of serious modification.

With such a winner on its hands the Great Western quickly ordered another three cars in 1934. Surprisingly these were not intended for branch lines but instead were for high-speed cross country duties for which purpose they were fitted with a lavatory and a small buffet, reducing the seating capacity to 40 people. Numbered 2-4 these railcars

entered service between Birmingham and Cardiff and two of the three were rostered for use each day. The three were constructed by AEC but this time C.B. Collett, Chief Mechanical Engineer of the GWR, took a keen interest, making several changes, not least the fitting of two engines in place of the one fitted to the earlier design. As a result the maximum speed went up to 75mph. Bodies were again by Park Royal.

These railcars were an instant hit with the public and stimulated traffic on the route so much that they were often inadequate for the number of passengers turning up to travel so steam locomotives and coaches had to substitute!

In 1935 there was again expansion of the railcar fleet when the GWR ordered three more, which became Nos 5-7. Although these were similar mechanically to Nos 2-4 they had bodies built by Gloucester Carriage and Wagon Company and were therefore to a revised design, there were 70 seats and the vehicles were 63ft 7in long and weighed 29tons 10cwt. Space was provided for luggage but this time there was no toilet or buffet counter. The cars were used in the Worcester and Oxford areas, mainly on feeder services into fast expresses to and from London.

Sheer confidence

By this time AEC had become so confident in the product that a new erecting shop for railcars was built at Southall which could house four cars at any one time. This faith was well justified for, even before Nos 5-7 had been delivered, the GWR ordered ten more streamliners in a bold move which was calculated to raise the amount of diesel mileage from 628 to 1,193 each day. The cars were to be used on 19 new services on lines ranging from Oxford to Hereford, Malvern to Birmingham and Worcester to Stratford-on-Avon. Again the bodywork was from the Gloucester Carriage and Wagon Co. Numbered 8-17 three were fitted with lavatories while six were not. The final vehicle was not equipped to carry passengers at all and was intended to be a dedicated parcels unit, for which purpose the body was amended to have no normal side windows but instead to have three sets of large sliding doors. This car was put to work between Reading and London where its duties included an early morning turn to Kensington to pick up Lyons Cakes. An important upgrade on these 10 cars was the replacement of the vacuum over hydraulic brake system with a conventional vacuum brake.

TABLE OF GWR RAILCARS

Car	Built	Withdrawn	Body	Chassis	Engine	Notes
1	1934	1955	Park Royal	Hardy/AEC	1xAEC 130hp	
2-4	1934	1954-8	Park Royal	AEC	2xAEC 130hp	
5-7	1935	1957-9	Gloucester	AEC	2xAEC 130hp	
8-16	1936	1956-60	Gloucester	AEC	2xAEC 130hp	No 9 withdrawn 1946 after fire
17	1936	1959	Gloucester	AEC	2xAEC 130hp	Parcels car
18	1937	1957	Gloucester	AEC	2xAEC 130hp	
19-33	1940-41	1960-62	Swindon	Swindon	2xAEC 105hp	33 rebuilt 1954 to replace 37
34	1941	1962	Swindon	Swindon	2xAEC 105hp	Parcels car
35-38	1941	1957-62	Swindon	Swindon	2xAEC 105hp	Two twin car sets No 37 withdrawn in 1947 due to fire

Notes - *Preserved: No 4 STEAM Museum, Swindon; No 20 Kent and East Sussex Railway (under restoration); No 22 Didcot Railway Centre (operational)*

Incremental development

The first 17 cars were not fitted with conventional couplings or buffing gear but had an attachment which would be used to clear the line in an emergency. Instead of buffers there were spring loaded pistons designed to take the load from any unintended impact. However from car No 18 onwards conventional buffers and drawgear were specified. This new vehicle featured a refined chassis, engines with a lower profile, five gears instead of four and bogie centres designed to give better riding.

An alteration which was to have great impact on the first generation DMUs was the adoption of pneumatic control, which later enabled multiple working to be developed. Again the body was by Gloucester and featured a revised design with what looked like a double-skinned roof to aid with ventilation. This vehicle could be operated with a trailer, and was often seen hauling autocoaches. Seating was provided for 49 with no toilet but a large luggage compartment with an exhaust-heated steam heat boiler being provided.

From No 19 onwards there was a radical departure from previous practice as this and all future cars were built at Swindon, with the works constructing the underframes, bogies and bodies. The design was based on No 18 and the cars were designed so that they could be worked in multiple with electro-pneumatic control. However the bodies were much more angular than the contractor-built ones and lost much of the streamlined feel of the earlier cars. Nos 19-33 were intended for branch line and local services and geared to run at 40mph, although two of them had dual range gears which enabled them to run at 60mph if required. The next vehicle, No 34, was a parcels car designed to assist No 17 while Nos 35-38 were built as two two-car units with only one cab at each end of each vehicle. These seated 104 per two-car set and had buffets and toilets and were designed for the Cardiff to Birmingham service where the capacity of the single cars was proving inadequate. Top speed was 75mph. These appeared in 1941 and were destined to be the last of these highly successful vehicles.

Spreading their wings

Immediately after the Second World War there was much interest in modernisation and the GWR cars were extensively trialled in other parts of the country, including Yorkshire and East Anglia. The first withdrawal was No 9 which caught fire in 1945, followed by No 37 which suffered a similar fate in 1947. A collision despatched No 2 in 1953 but the rest survived long enough to be replaced by first generation DMUs between 1954 and 1962. Three have been preserved. When owned by the GWR the livery was chocolate and cream but this was changed to crimson and cream following nationalisation and later to standard BR maroon.

The Great Western railcars accurately predicted much of the mechanical layout of the later British Railways DMUs. Most first-generation units shared the principle of having two AEC/Leyland engines driving a Wilson epicyclic gearbox with two cars coupled together using vacuum brakes and electro-pneumatic control. Despite being initially thought of as experimental vehicles all had a long and successful life, yet at the time they were designed very little was known about railcar design for railway use. That the concept was such a success is a huge tribute to the forward-thinking designers at the Hardy Motors Works in Southall, who produced this revolutionary design almost 80 years ago.

W33 was built as a single car unit in 1941 but rebuilt in 1954 to replace W37 in a two car set after it caught fire in 1947. The two car set rests at Worcester on an unknown date. Colour Rail.

Signalling
the branch

Signalling on a layout is often something of an afterthought but, as **Evan Green-Hughes** explains, getting this aspect right can add a great deal to the authenticity of a railway scene.

How many times have you been to an exhibition and looked at layouts which are seemingly perfect but somehow lack that certain ring of authenticity? Buildings, scenery and the trains themselves are often the result of painstaking research and extensive work but the signals are often illogically placed and non-operational. Worse still are the numbers of trains driven past signals which are firmly set at danger, further detracting from the overall impression of the layout. The effect is subtle but crucial: if signals are installed in unrealistic locations the illusion of realism we all try so hard to achieve is shattered.

However by doing a little research it's easy to both site and use signalling correctly and in the process to make the layout look that bit more like the real thing. We've set out to look at one of the most commonly modelled areas, the branch line, and find out what sort of signalling would typically be installed.

Little signalling

The simplest form of branch line, surprisingly, may have no signals at all and would be worked on the one engine in steam principle by which the driver of a train accessing the branch at the junction would be given a staff, tablet or token. These can take many forms, from complicated metal types to simple pieces of wood but all would be clearly marked with the section of line to which they relate. The token gives the driver authority over the branch and while his train is there then no other can be admitted.

It follows that with this system signals are not necessary, except where the branch joins the main line. There you would expect to find a distant signal, warning of the junction approach, followed by a stop signal guarding the junction itself. Usually there would also be a stop signal which would allow access to the branch and this was more often than not interlocked with a token instrument in the signalbox so that it could only be cleared once each time the token was withdrawn, therefore providing an additional safeguard. There are a few such examples on the present day network: the Gunnislake branch is token worked from St Budeaux Victoria Road on the one engine in steam principle, amongst others.

From the modeller's point of view it is worth remembering that where there are no signals there should not be a signalbox but where there are sidings or run round loops there would be a ground frame into which the token would be put to release the points.

Demanding movement

Obviously there were not many branches where one train could cope with the demand for both passengers and goods and so most would have been provided with at least one signalbox with attendant signals. Where the line was short a 'box was most commonly provided at the end and in most cases the layout was very similar. As a train approached the terminus the first signal that would be seen would be the distant. This was a yellow arm with a fishtail end with black markings. The purpose of this signal was to warn of a stop signal ahead

and the actual location and distance from the stop signal would be dictated by the line speed and by the geography of the area. Typically, though, a quarter of a mile was not uncommon, a distance which would have to be shortened to get this signal into most layouts.

The next signal which would be encountered would be the station's home signal. The home is the first stop signal controlled by a signalbox in any particular direction, and the term should not be used for any other sort of stop signal. This signal would have the familiar

Midland Railway '1P' 0-4-4T 58065 passes the home and distant signal as it leaves Southwell with the push pull train for Rolleston Junction on September 30 1957. Gordon Hepburn/Rail Archive Stephenson.

red arm, square at the end, and with a white stripe and would be placed sufficiently far from the station to enable an incoming train to be held well away from any shunting moves or possible causes of conflict.

In all but the smallest termini there would have been a second stop signal controlling access to the platform, which in the case of a dead-end line would be pulled off just as the train reached it to indicate to the driver that he must stop ahead.

A train leaving the platform to return

down the branch would expect to see the stop signal at the end of the platform, usually called the starter, to be pulled off and after the immediate area of the station is left behind there would be another stop signal, hopefully in the 'Off' position, which tells the driver that the train is clear to enter the section ahead. From this point on the driver would also need to be in possession of a staff or token which would have been given to him by the signalman before he set out, or collected from the signalbox on the way past, as this signal would

mark the end of the area controlled by the signalbox at the terminus.

To control entry to sidings and run round loops the station would also be equipped with small signals, known as 'subsidiaries', 'dummies' or 'dods' depending on when and where you were trained. These are most commonly found in the form of a white disc with a red line across, which when in the normal position means stop but when rotated so that the line is diagonal mean proceed with caution as far as the line is clear. Even the smallest branch terminus would have these and they would be used, for instance, when running an engine round a train to signal to the driver that the platform was already occupied.

Subsidiary signals are read from top to bottom referring to routes left to right, so if three subsidiaries were provided one on top of the other and the top one was off this indicates that the left-hand route is to be taken. Other forms of these signals include small semaphore arms and the modern triangular ground colour light signal. Rarely modelled, these signals were an important part of the safe running of any branch terminus and add a surprising amount of authenticity to any scene.

Where two or more passenger platforms were provided it would be necessary to provide a bracket signal or similar to instruct the driver as to which route he was to take. Where one signal post on a bracket is higher than another this indicates to a driver which is the main route, so in your typical branch terminus the normal arrival platform would likely have the taller bracket arm.

Passing loops

Where the branch was longer or where a passing place was provided along its length then another signalbox would be provided at an intermediate point and a distant and home provided at each end in each direction. Leaving the station would be a starter and then a section signal, however where a goods yard was provided, or where trains could work both directions through each platform you might find that more signals would

be provided.

To proceed onto a single line section tokens would have to be exchanged, the signalman receiving them from the driver and only allowing them to move forwards when he had the token for that section. Trains often passed at these locations, and the rule was generally but not always 'first in, last out'. This was because the signalman could hand the token given to him by the first train to the second as it arrived. He would then take the token from the second train, ensure that the line ahead was clear and give it to the first train which entered the loop. It's an easy way of justifying having two trains in what would otherwise be a fairly quiet station.

Colour lights

Examples of branch lines equipped with colour light signals are much rarer due to closures but the principle still remained the same. The distant signal would be a two-aspect colour light which could show either yellow or green (although distants approaching terminus stations are usually fixed at 'caution') and the stop signals would all be capable of showing a red or a green aspect. However the bracket signal gave way to signals which can show routes differently, one example at a terminus being the 'theatre indicator' which gives a driver a proceed aspect together with the number of the platform or track to which he is being directed. On modern branches as the terminus is invariably a single platform, this is largely irrelevant, but not always.

Modernisation changed the face of

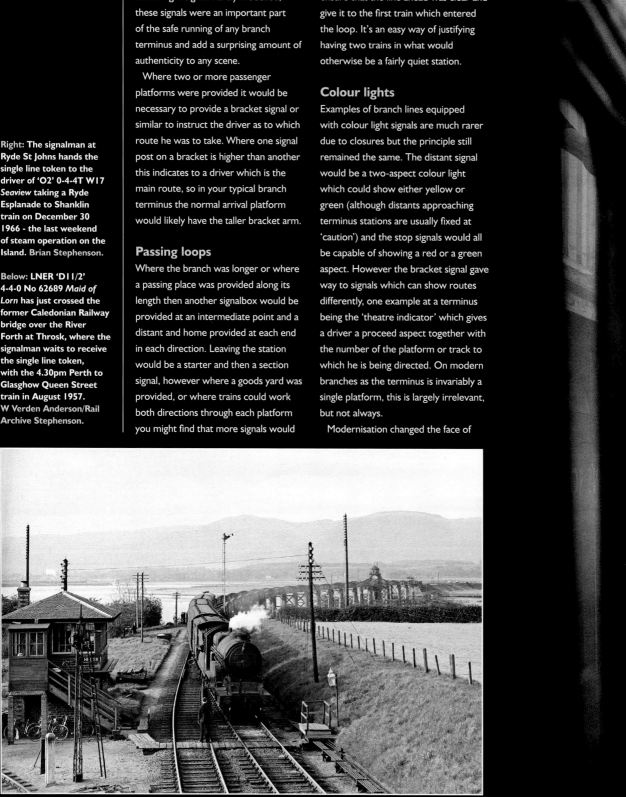

signalling. In most cases single line tokens were done away with in favour of track circuits or 'change direction' levers. In the former, electronic circuits tell the signalman where the train is and prevent another being admitted to the same section and in the latter the signalmen at each end agree on which direction the trains will run and both operate a lever which allows the signals to clear in only one direction. From the modellers' point of view these changes mean that there is no reason to provide token catchers and set down posts outside your signalboxes and the token instruments can be omitted from signal box interiors. The 'boxes themselves disappeared steadily from the 1950s onwards but often where they stood you will find a collection of location cabinets and perhaps evidence of the signalbox foundations. Of course by the 1980s many of the branches which survived were freight only and many had no signalling at all.

Those modelling the up-to-date branch line scene may not have to worry too much about signals. Much of rural Scotland is operated on the Radio Electronic Token Block system which provides for drivers to receive tokens by radio into special equipment fitted in their cabs. However there are stop boards to be modelled at the end of every token section and at the end of every passing loop, more or less in the places where the stop signals used to be, and there are many location cabinets containing

equipment as well as the radio masts which provide the radio signals. Stop boards will also be found protecting level crossings where there will also be a white flashing light signal provided so that an approaching train driver can be assured that the flashing red road lights have worked correctly and that the barriers, if fitted, are down.

Bang up to date

On the Cambrian Coast lines fixed signals are now a thing of the past with the installation of the latest European Rail Traffic Management System (ERTMS) equipment and drivers receive all their instructions by means of screens fitted to the cabs of traction units so in the future there may not be a requirement for modellers of the truly modern scene to provide any signals at all, presenting yet another variation to the story of signalling.

As always with railways there are many variations in the way that signals can be provided and because of this there is no substitute for accurate research of the prototype. However by following the general principles set out here you can devise a reasonably accurate scheme for any layout, whether based on a fictional place or an actual location. Once you have working signals in place you will be surprised by how much fun you can have accurately signalling every train and you, too, will wince every time you see a model passing a signal at danger!

Above: The fireman of 'K1/1' 61997 *MacCailin Mor* takes the single line tablet from the signalman at Fort William as it leaves with a train for Mallaig in June 1954. Note the school boy assisting! Eric Fry/Rail Archive Stephenson.

Left: Capturing a typical Western Region branch working GWR '43XX' 2-6-0 7303 leaves Venn Cross with the 10.12am Ilfracombe to Paddington train on June 27 1964. Mike Fox/Rail Archive Stephenson.

Operation
and rolling stock

The signal drops, the regulator opens and the first train finally runs on St Stephens Road, but how can get the most enjoyment out of your creation? **Andrew Roden** and **Mike Wild** examine some of the possibilities and discuss the locomotives and rolling stock which operate on this new exhibition layout. *Photography, Mike Wild.*

A Collett '2251' 0-6-0 slows on the approach to St Stephens Road where it is signalled into the goods loop. Here the locomotive will shunt its pick up goods to the yard where wagons will be exchanged.

With any luck there comes a point in every model railway where the list of 'big jobs' to complete runs out, to be replaced by smaller, optional tasks. And oddly, just at the moment where the satisfaction should be greatest, for many modellers, that moment of completion is curiously hollow.

For some, to be sure, the most satisfaction is gained from building the model railway itself but given that most of us build a layout with the express purpose of operating it, it makes sense that we should seek to enjoy that process to the full. Now, there's nothing wrong with *ad hoc* operation (or, if you prefer, playing with trains), and it would be a rare modeller who doesn't indulge in this during the construction phase. When the layout is complete, however, operation without any forethought is rarely satisfying for long. A well thought through operating plan is very often the factor which transforms a layout from a beautifully detailed trainset into a fully fledged model railway.

There are three distinct approaches to achieving this, all with their own advantages and disadvantages.

Run what's next

The simplest way of structuring an operating session is to use the approach of St Stephens Road's sister project layout Berrybridge. Here, the trains are loaded into the fiddle yards in the order that they are due to run in, so you might run the nearest train in the left-hand fiddle yard first into the furthest away track in the right-hand yard, and once that's entered the

ST STEPHENS LOCOMOTIVE FLEET

Locomotive	Manufacturer	Availability
Western Region		
Collett '14XX' 0-4-2T	Hornby	Current
Collett '57XX' 0-6-0PT	Bachmann	Current
Collett '8750' 0-6-0PT	Bachmann	Current
Churchward '45XX' 2-6-2T	Bachmann	Current
Collett '4575' 2-6-2T	Bachmann	Current
Collett '2251' 0-6-0	Bachmann	Due 2011
Collett 'Hall' 4-6-0	Bachmann	Current
Churchward '28XX' 2-8-0	Hornby	Current
'Warship' B-B	Bachmann	Current
'Hymek' Bo-Bo	Heljan	Current
'Western' C-C	Heljan	Current
GWR Railcar	Hornby	Current
Southern Region		
Drummond 'M7' 0-4-4T	Hornby	Current
Maunsell 'N' 2-6-0	Bachmann	Current
Drummond 'T9' 4-4-0	Hornby	Current
Riddles '4MT' 2-6-0	Bachmann	Current
Bulleid 'West Country' 4-6-2	Hornby	Current
Beattie '0298' 2-4-0WT	Kernow MRC	Current

ST STEPHENS ROAD PASSENGER FORMATIONS

Formation	Manufacturer
Western Region	
Three coach BR maroon Hawksworth set	Hornby
Three coach BR carmine and cream Mk I set	Bachmann
Three coach BR maroon Collett set	Bachmann
BR carmine and cream Autocoach	Hornby
BR maroon Autocoach	Hornby
BR carmine GWR B-set	Hornby
Five coach BR Mk I rake	Bachmann
Southern Region	
Three coach BR green Mk I set	Bachmann
Three coach BR green Bulleid set	Bachmann
Three coach BR green Maunsell set	Hornby
Two coach BR green Maunsell set	Hornby

opposite end, run the nearest train on the right-hand side into the vacant track at the opposite end and so on.

This has the great advantage that it's simple to set up and vary, and you can do it from the very first moment you begin operating your layout. The disadvantage is that although it's a more formal approach to operating it doesn't explicitly set out a purpose for each train, so while ideal for exhibitions where train movements need to be frequent, its appeal can wane at home.

Defined sequence

A step up from simply running what's next in the fiddle yard is to plan a typical 'day's traffic for the railway and incorporate it in a written operating plan. The day might start, for example, with a local passenger train for early rising workers, connecting with an autocoach on the branch platform. Then there might be a pick up goods heading in the opposite direction, pausing to marshal some wagons from the goods yard before shuffling on. Then there could be another passenger train, followed by china clay empties for sending up the branch, and so on.

The great thing with this approach is that by forcing you to think about a reasonably realistic operation, the moves you make magically become more enjoyable. Because every train now has a purpose (even if in reality all it does is move from one fiddle yard to another), it fits in with a wider picture. There's

any number of ways of doing it, from having cards with the various trains on and shuffling them to provide the day's timetable to having a formal plan and everywhere in between.

One of the nicest things about doing this is that although it imposes order it doesn't impose a deadline, so if you want to spend a while shunting the wagons in the goods yard into alphabetical order you can.

Similarly, if you want to introduce a little variety to things, perhaps with a different locomotive or a special working, there's nothing to stop this happening. Providing you can come back to the operating plan at some point, then it will work out really well and make an enjoyable layout to run.

The timetable approach

For purists, even an operating sequence isn't quite enough, and the next step is something which approximates even more closely to real operation. Clearly, adhering to real time would mean that most of the operating time would be spent waiting for trains, but by speeding a clock so that, for example, one minute in real time equals five in model time and working out a practical timetable, it is surprising just how absorbing this approach can be.

Where a model railway has two or more stations, timetabled operation is more attractive still as some skill has to be exercised in ensuring trains don't arrive too early or late. When this might involve some complex shunting or

running round, it's almost like a game in its own right. The disadvantage, of course, is that planning the timetable takes a lot longer than generating an operating sequence, but it's still feasible and enjoyable.

Fun with friends

Achieving a degree of realistic operation is one of the most important aspects of enjoying a model railway, but so too is sharing it with friends. Thankfully, Digital Command Control makes operating multiple trains much simpler than its DC equivalent, and with two or more controllers there is scope for some really intensive operations, with one operator controlling the branch, another the main line and one more the goods yard. The

 Above: With the route through St Stephens being single track goods trains are often held in the loop to allow a passenger working to pass. A 'Warship' hydraulic prepares to restart from the station while a 'Small Prairie' waits in the middle goods loop.

 Left: With the signal 'off' a Drummond 'M7' eases a short passenger working away from St Stephens on the Southern Region route.

communication and liaison needed to keep things operating smoothly can be a challenge, but as any exhibitor will confirm, it's often when communication breaks down that running a model railway is at its most entertaining. Trying to extract the trains from an operating tangle without resorting to the Great Hand From The Sky can be uproarious fun!

Bringing friends round, swapping yarns and playing trains is probably the single best way of enjoying your model railway of all. If they bring their own stock round to add some variety, so much the better, and if it's not strictly appropriate for the

layout, well, that's part of the fun too.

How else can you get the most out of your model railway? Exhibiting it is an obvious way if the layout is portable, and you don't need to be aiming for the National Model Railway Exhibition at the NEC.

As well as model railway clubs (and you're unlikely to be far from one) all sorts of local organisations have events where model railways can be exhibited. The local church raising funds for its roof, village fetes, fundraisers for community groups - all may welcome a model

railway or two if they think they will attract visitors. The non-specialist groups can often be a good way of dipping your toes in the waters of exhibiting in a less pressured way than an exhibition.

If you can't exhibit your model railway there's no reason not to share it with others via the internet. A whole host of web forums exist for modellers to share their creations on, and if the sometimes intense atmosphere of the forums isn't quite for you, why not create a weblog? Again, there are a host of options, but it's a free and easy way of showcasing

your model railway and getting to know likeminded modellers.

For some modellers, completing a model railway is the end of a journey, but for us, it's more like changing trains onto another route entirely - an altogether different experience, but one which is every bit as enjoyable as the build itself.

Stocking St Stephens

Rolling stock can make or break a model railway. Moving back to our subject layout, St Stephens Road, we've set the period as the transition from steam to diesel traction with a focus on Western Region motive power and stock. This is augmented by the Southern Region route which uses the same station forming the pinnacle of the layout.

There is always room for manoeuvre in a locomotive fleet and this is no more true than in St Stephens Road's allocation. While the majority of the locomotives chosen are totally appropriate for the area modelled, some push the boundaries of reality. However, while authenticity is always important, sometimes personal favourites lead to a little modellers license and there is no harm in that.

For St Stephens Road there are two main anomalies – a GWR AEC railcar and a GWR '28XX' 2-8-0. Neither of these classes had associations with Cornwall, but for me personally they are what I like and I'm prepared to push the boundaries a little to incorporate them.

Similarly the time period covered by the fleet is a little broader than perhaps it should be. For the layout there is a varied fleet of steam and diesel classes covering examples of the Collett '14XX' 0-4-2T, Churchward and Collett 2-6-2Ts, Collett 'Hall' 4-6-0 and Collett '2251' 0-6-0 plus hydraulic diesels – another personal favourite subject of mine – in the form of 'Warships', 'Hymeks' and a 'Western' too for good measure.

[O]5 **Left: The station area can become very busy with arriving and departing trains. A BR lined black '45XX' restarts its train on the Western following the arrival of a loaded china clay train while an 'M7' pauses in the platform for the Southern Region.**

[O]6 **Below: A Collett '4575' 2-6-2T take the junction onto the Southern Region route with a rake of china clay wagons. These will be taken to the nearby clay dries for loading before returning to St Stephens and, ultimately, a dock on the South Cornwall coast.**

A Collett 'Hall' 4-6-0 approaches St Stephens with a passenger working. In the station a Maunsell 'N' 2-6-0 waits to depart with a Southern Region passenger working while in the goods yard a Collett '2251' shuffles wagons for its goods train.

Some of these are difficult to justify for a branch line, but I will attempt to make a reason for all.

Operating the fleet

The Western Region operation has 16 locomotives available together with seven passenger formations and a choice of 10 goods trains – the latter being split between the Western and Southern operations.

The majority of the passenger trains are formed of three coach sets consisting of Hawksworth, Collett and BR Mk I coaches. There are also two Autocoaches and an ex-GWR 'B-set'. These trains form a mixture of branch trains and through trains. Locomotives allocated to these trains include a pair of 'Warship' diesel hydraulics, a Churchward '45XX' and

Collett '4575' 2-6-2T and a 'Hall' 4-6-0. The Autocoaches are in the hands of a pair of Collett '14XX' 0-4-2Ts.

The seventh passenger formation for the Western arm of St Stephens Road is a five coach through train which runs non-stop – unless held for a passing freight

ST STEPHENS ROAD FREIGHT FORMATIONS

Formation	Route
Box vans	Southern Region
China clay (two sets)	Western/Southern
Mixed goods (Four sets)	Western/Southern
Fuel train	Western
Cattle	Western
Ballast	Western/Southern

– to the coastal terminus of the line carrying holidaymakers to and from their resorts. This is in the hands of the largest

locomotives permitted on the branch with the choice of a 'Western' diesel hydraulic, 'Hall' or 'Castle' 4-6-0s.

The Southern Region route through St Stephens Road has its own dedicated set of passenger trains. These consist of three coach sets using Maunsell, Bulleid and BR Mk I vehicles. All of these are decorated in BR Southern Region green which helps further the operation and understanding of two routes running through St Stephens. The passenger trains are in the hands of Drummond 'T9' 4-4-0s, Bulleid 'West Country' 4-6-2s and Maunsell 'N' 2-6-0s.

On the freight side the combination of freights moving between the two routes makes for interesting operation. The Southern Region freights consist, in the main, of box vans, pick up goods and a dedicated ballast train. These are hauled by a wider selection of locomotives including Drummond 'M7' 0-4-4Ts, Maunsell 'N' 2-6-0s and BR '4MT' 2-6-0s. The pick up goods trains set back onto Western Region metals to drop off and collect wagons providing an interchange for these important freight flows.

At exhibitions we will operate St Stephens through the 'run what's next' process by having a range of trains arranged in the fiddle yards to provide an interesting sequence. This sequence is then broken by trains changing between regions. The china clay trains, for example, originate on the Western

route and transfer to Southern metals to reach the nearby clay dries while pick up goods trains from the Southern use the crossover to reach the yard.

However you choose to operate your layout there are plenty of options available to make it both interesting and entertaining. Developing reasons for freight flows will help advance operating practise too.

We hope you have enjoyed reading about St Stephens Road. Keep an eye on *Hornby Magazine* to find out when and where we will be exhibiting this new layout.

A '57XX' 0-6-0PT draws to a halt in the goods loop, clearing the line for the '14XX' and autocoach.

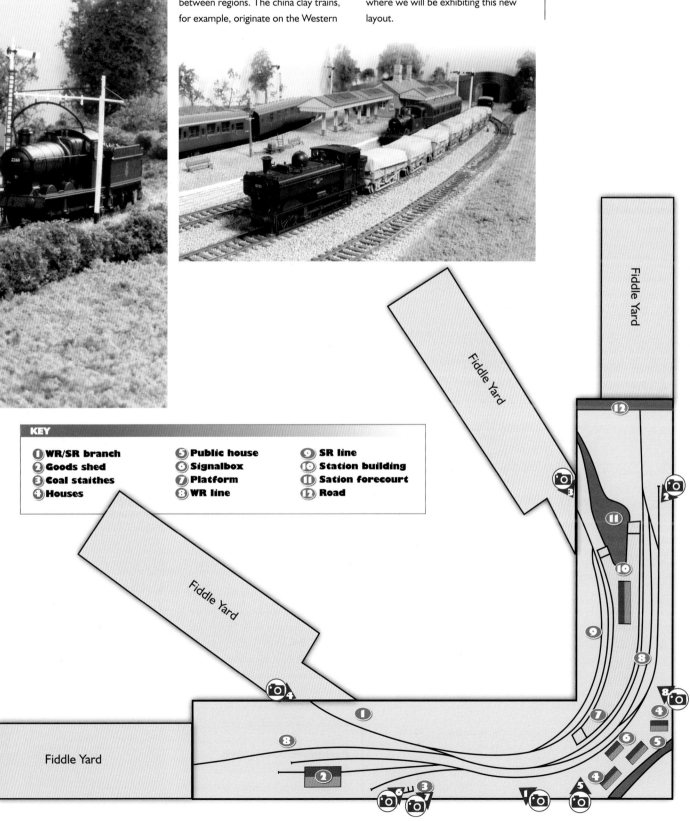

KEY

1. WR/SR branch
2. Goods shed
3. Coal staithes
4. Houses
5. Public house
6. Signalbox
7. Platform
8. WR line
9. SR line
10. Station building
11. Sation forecourt
12. Road

Fiddle Yard

Fiddle Yard

Fiddle Yard

Fiddle Yard

Forward to 2012

The past 12 months have witnessed a tremendous range of new locomotives entering the ready-to-run market, but what else is in store? **Mike Wild** looks forward to the end of 2011 and 2012 to round up what will be next in 'N', 'OO' and 'O' gauge.

NEW 'OO' READY-TO-RUN LOCOMOTIVES 2011-2012

Model	Manufacturer	Release date
GWR 'Dukedog' 4-4-0	Bachmann	2012
SECR 'C' class 0-6-0	Bachmann	2012
Midland '3F' 0-6-0	Bachmann	December 2011
GWR ROD '3000' 2-8-0	Bachmann	December 2011
Blue Pullman DEMU	Bachmann	2012
Derby Lightweight DMU	Bachmann	December 2011
Class 85 Bo-Bo	Bachmann	2012
Class 350 Desiro EMU	Bachmann	2012
LMS twins 10000/10001	Bachmann	2012
Class 22 B-B	Dapol	September 2011
Class 52 C-C	Dapol	December 2011
Class 21/29 Bo-Bo	Dapol	2012
Gresley 'B17' 4-6-0	Hornby	October 2011
Thompson 'B1' 4-6-0	Hornby	November 2011
'Brighton Belle' 5-BEL EMU	Hornby	2012
Class 23 'Baby Deltic'	Heljan	December 2011
Waggon und Machinenbau railbus	Heljan	December 2011
AC Cars railbus	Heljan	2012
Class 128 DMU	Heljan	2012
English Electric prototype DP2	Heljan	December 2011
Class 76 EM1 Bo-Bo	Olivia's Trains/Heljan	September 2011
Class 77 EM2 Co-Co	Olivia's Trains/Heljan	2012
LMS 10000/10001	Hatton's/Dapol	2011
Class 28 Co-Bo	Hatton's/Heljan	September 2011
LMS Beyer, Garratt 2-6-0+0-6-2	Hatton's/Heljan	December 2012
Adams 'O2' 0-4-4T	Kernow MRC/Dapol	2012
Bulleid 10201-10203	Kernow MRC/Dapol	2012
D600 series Warship	Kernow MRC/Dapol	2012
Class 205 2H DEMU	Kernow MRC/Bachmann	2012
Class 143 DMU	Realtrack Models	2012
Class 144 DMU	Realtrack Models	2012
Class 33/0 Bo-Bo	Rail Exclusive/Heljan	2012

What do you get when you add together six mainstream manufacturers, five retailers and three scales? The answer is 51 new locomotive and multiple unit models which are due to be released within the next 18 months!

The phrase 'we've never had it so good' is something of a cliché now, but never before has this been more true of the model railway market. Our manufacturers are pushing harder than ever before to bring us more of what we want and by the bucket load too.

'OO' and 'N' gauge are the biggest winners in the list of new products as there are currently only a handful of 'O' gauge ready-to-run locomotive due for release in 2012. However, take a look at the list and see what's on offer – how does a Midland '3F' 0-6-0 or a 'Brighton Belle' EMU sound? Not enough? How about a Woodhead Class 76 or maybe a LMS Beyer, Garratt 2-6-0+0-6-2 sound?

All of these have been announced and are at varying stages of planning, design and production, but they are all on the cards for release between September 2011 and through 2012. It is a list which I don't think anyone could have predicted even 12 months ago, but such is the ability of manufacturers and the ever growing commission market that anything is now possible.

Bachmann 'OO' gauge

Bachmann is charging through an impressive range of product promises

and many of these are either lower order classes or unusual prototypes with limited geographical spheres. However, it doesn't stop these models having a great chance of success.

The highlights for steam era modellers are undoubtedly the GWR 'Dukedog' 4-4-0 and SECR Wainwright 'C' class 0-6-0. Both of these were announced at the annual 2011 catalogue launch in March 2011 with the intention that both will be in the shops during 2012. Beyond this Bachmann is also jumping the last hurdles to produce a Midland '3F' 0-6-0 with a release date of December 2011/ January 2012 and the GWR ROD '3000' 2-8-0 which is due out in December 2011. Both of these models were in the process of production as this Yearbook closed for press in early September.

However, it is multiple units which are benefitting the most at Bachmann. Due out are the Southern Region Class 419 Motor Luggage Van, Derby Lightweight DMU, Class 350 Desiro EMU and, perhaps the most significant, the Blue Pullman Diesel Electric Multiple Unit.

In terms of locomotives Bachmann is producing a Class 85 with three different body detail variants and it is also working hand in hand with Rails of Sheffield to produce LMS twins 10000 and 10001 with the BR green liveried models being offered as catalogue releases and the LMS and BR black versions being exclusive to Rails.

Hornby 'OO' gauge

Over at Hornby's headquarters production is a little quieter, but no less impressive. Due for release before the end of 2011 is the delayed Gresley 'B17' 4-6-0 which will produced as a 'B17/1', 'B17/2' and 'B17/6' with capacity in the toolings for detail differences in the boiler and two styles of tender.

A second LNER offering due in November 2011 is a brand new model of the Thompson 'B1' 4-6-0. This mixed traffic locomotive was prolific on the Eastern Region and will feature a new permanent coupling between the locomotive and tender.

The icing on the cake for Hornby though is the 'Brighton Belle' 5-BEL EMU. This is advancing rapidly through the production process, but its release has been held back to the first half of 2012 to allow more detailed work to be carried on the unit. This will be produced in both Pullman umber and cream and BR blue and grey liveries with the motor cars being sold as a twin pack and the three centre trailer vehicles being launched as individual vehicles.

Heljan 'OO' gauge

Over the water in Denmark the team at Heljan is working on some impressive

Right: Hattons has announced one of the most impressive locomotives to run in the UK in the LMS Beyer, Garratt 2-6-0+0-6-2. In May 1956 ex-LMS Garratt 47988 takes water at Wellingborough shed. Stephen Summerson/ Rail Archive Stephenson.

models of its own as well as meeting the demands of commissioners Olivias Trains and Hattons.

In Heljan's own schedule are the Class 23 'Baby Deltic' which is due to be released in December 2011 and the Waggon und Machinenbau railbus which is also due to go on sale before the end of 2011.

These two fine models will be followed by the AC Cars diesel railbus, the Class 128 Gloucester diesel parcels unit and unique English Electric prototype DP2. DP2 was progressing through the pre-production process in late summer 2011 with the release date planned for late 2011 or early 2012.

Dapol 'OO' gauge

Dapol is due to re-enter the 'OO' gauge ready-to-run market during the autumn of 2011 with its delayed model of the North British Locomotives Class 22 diesel hydraulic. This is its first home grown foray into ready-to-run 'OO' gauge locomotives, although it follows two highly successful commissions from Kernow Model Rail Centre and *Model Rail* with the Beattie '0298' 2-4-0WT and Sentinel 4wVBT respectively.

However, after the Class 22 Dapol is also working on a brand new model of the Class 52 Western hydraulic which is earmarked for release before the end of 2011 as well as the NBL Class 21/29. A model of DP2 had been announced by Dapol, but this has now been shelved to allow Heljan to continue with its project.

The commissioners

However, while the 'OO' gauge manufacturers are already busy with its own projects there is a second avenue which is growing the availability of ready-to-run locomotives – the commission market.

Kernow Model Rail Centre has been at the head of this since 2008 when it announced it would be producing a model of the BR Class 205 DEMU with Dapol. Production has now switched to Bachmann which will allow for the provision to fit the models with DCC sound and also the use of the high quality front end design work done for the Bachmann 2-EPB.

Kernow had just released the first versions of its Dapol produced Beattie 2-4-0WT as this Yearbook closed for press, but it is also working on models of the Adams 'O2' 0-4-4T, Bulleid diesels 10201-10203 and the NBL D600 series Warships. The latter three models are expected to be released in 2012. Hattons is another major player in the commission market. Its first venture was a Class 14 diesel hydraulic with Heljan and this is being followed by the Class 28 Co-Bo diesel electric which is scheduled to arrive in the UK in September 2011.

The Liverpool based retailer is also working with Dapol to produce models of the LMS prototype diesels 10000/10001 and is making great strides in incorporating the huge number of detail variations in the two locomotives during their careers so that a full range can be produced.

However, Hatton's greatest hit is without doubt the news that it will be producing the LMS Beyer, Garratt 2-6-0+0-6-2 with Heljan for release in 2012. The company announced this model in August 2011 and is planning to have it ready for December 2012.

Rails of Sheffield is working with Bachmann to produce LMS twins 10000/10001 while Olivia's Trains is nearing completion of its project to manufacturer the Woodhead electric Class 76 EM1 Bo-Bo with Heljan – release is expected in September 2011. Olivias is also working on the Class 77 EM2 Co-Co electric with Heljan and this

NEW 'N' READY-TO-RUN LOCOMOTIVES 2011-2012

Model	Manufacturer	Release date
Peppercorn 'A1' 4-6-2	Bachmann	September 2011
BR 'Standard Five' 4-6-0	Bachmann	2012
Gresley 'J39' 0-6-0	Bachmann	2012
Riddles 'WD' 2-8-0	Bachmann	2012
Ivatt '2MT' 2-6-0	Bachmann	2012
Class 03 0-6-0	Bachmann	September 2011
Class 08 0-6-0 (original condition)	Bachmann	2012
Class 20 Bo-Bo	Bachmann	2012
Class 350 Desiro EMU	Bachmann	2012
Class 411 4-CEP EMU	Bachmann	2012
Blue Pullman DEMU	Bachmann	2012
Class 26 Bo-Bo	Dapol	September 2011
Class 52 C-C	Dapol	2011
Class 56 Co-Co	Dapol	2011
Class 121 DMU	Dapol	2012
Class 142 DMU	Dapol	2012
GWR '43XX' 2-6-0	Ixion Models	2012

is on the cards for 2012.

Rail Exclusive is also working with Heljan to produce a brand new body tooling for the Class 33/0 in original condition which will have a corrected cab roof profile and accurate roof details. This model will be sold in twin packs with release expected in 2012.

Elsewhere Realtrack Models is due to receive its ready-to-run Class 144 DMUs in 2012 followed closely by the similar, but equally different, Class 143 DMUs. These follow on from its success of producing the FLA container flats and the DMUs will follow suit in being produced entirely independently.

The Table on page 124 details all of the ready-to-run locomotives which have been announced for 'OO' gauge.

'N' gauge flourishes

'OO' gauge manufacturer is naturally very busy, but 'N' gauge modellers are in line for no less than 16 new locomotive and multiple unit models in the coming months.

Bachmann's Graham Farish arm is leading the way with 11 new items in the offing with release dates ranging from September 2011 through to the end of 2012. These include the Peppercorn 'A1' 4-6-2 and Class 03 diesel shunter which were due to arrive in the UK imminently in early September followed by the BR 'Standard Five' 4-6-0, 'WD' 2-8-0, Gresley 'J39' and Ivatt '2MT'. The BR 4-6-0 will feature a new locomotive drive mechanism for a Bachmann 'N' gauge steam locomotive too.

In the diesel stakes multiple units are a high priority with the Class 350 Desiro, Class 411 4-CEP EMU and Blue Pullman all on the cards from Bachmann. Similarly Dapol is working on models of the Class 121 single car DMU and the Class 142 two-car diesel railbus.

Diesel locomotives haven't been ignored though as Bachmann is working on a brand new Class 20 for 'N' gauge as well as an original condition version of the Class 08 diesel shunter. Meanwhile Dapol's first all new Class 26 arrived in the *Hornby Magazine* office in early

September and it will be followed by a Class 52 and Class 56 for 'N' too.

'O' gauge is also quietly progressing with Heljan having released its Class 55 production 'Deltic' in September which will be followed in 2012 by the Class 31 A1A-A1A diesel electric. However, it shouldn't be forgotten that premium 'O' gauge manufacturers Golden Age Models are working on a Peppercorn 'A1' and 'A2' as well as a 'Merchant Navy' for 'O' gauge.

Something for everyone

With such a broad spectrum of locomotives being offered in the coming months there will be something for everyone. What we have here is a truly stunning line up and one which is set to grow again in the New Year as Hornby and Bachmann reveal their catalogues and plans for 2012 and beyond.

This really is a very exciting time for railway modellers of all scales and it is heartening to see the hobby grow and grow. The question is, as always, what's next!

Above: Bachmann's Blue Pullman is expected to be released during 2012. The Birmingham Pullman enters London Paddington in September 1962. Lewis Coles/ Rail Archive Stephenson.

Top left: Olivias Trains commissioned model of the EM1 Bo-Bo electric was expected to arrive in the shops during September 2011. In 1955 EM1 26014 banks a coal train from Wath past Oxspring Junction signalbox. Kenneth Field/Rail Archive Stephenson.

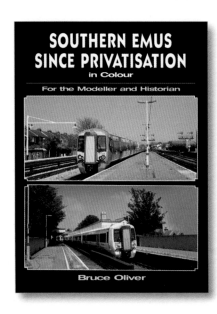